CONT

Exploring
Mount Helena

Edited by
Erin Turner & Ric Bourie

FALCON®
Helena, Montana

AFALCONGUIDE®

Falcon® is continually expanding its list of books. You can order extra copies of this book and get information and prices for other Falcon books by writing Falcon, P.O. Box 1718, Helena, MT 59624, or calling 1-800-582-2665. Please ask for a free copy of our current catalog listing all Falcon books.

To contact us via e-mail, visit our home page http://www.falconguide.com

Printed in Canada

Cover photos by John Reddy.

Plant illustrations on pages 59 and 60 reprinted from Hitchcock, et al. *Vascular Plants of the Pacific Northwest*, Seattle: University of Washington Press.

Library of Congress Cataloging-in-Publication Data
Exploring Mount Helena / edited by Erin Turner and Ric Bourie.
       p. cm.
    Includes bibliographical references (p.).
    ISBN 1-56044-524-6 (pbk.)
      1. Mount Helena City Park (Helena, Mont.)—Juvenile literature.
    2. Helena (Mont.)—Description and travel—Juvenile literature.
    I. Turner, Erin.
    II. Bourie, Richard.
    F739.H4E97 1997
    917.86'615—dc21
                                     97-20017
                                          CIP

♻ Text pages printed on recycled paper.

ACKNOWLEDGMENTS

———◆———

The idea for this book was conceived by the employees of Falcon as a community service project. They have donated many hours of staff time to this book, as a part of the continued effort to maintain Mount Helena City Park for the use and enjoyment of the citizens of Helena. They were joined in this effort by hardworking volunteers from the community who contributed their time and effort to the chapters contained here, Gayle Joslin, Wayne Phillips, Bonnie Heidel, Joe Elliott, Dan Sullivan, Bea Vogel, Ray Breuninger, and Bill Schneider.

Randy Lilje, Ellen Sievert, Chere Jiusto, the Montana Historical Society, Christian Sarver, and John Reddy deserve special thanks for their help in putting the book together, as well.

———◆———

All profits from the sale of this book go toward the preservation or expansion of Mount Helena as a unique city park.

Mount Helena, December 1972. Wayne Philips photo.

INTRODUCTION

◆

Mount Helena is a passive participant in and benign witness to Helena's history. Every day the mountain sits stoically on the edge of Montana's capital city, presiding over the human activity at its base, and casting glances across the valley below. The same mass of rock that loomed over the "Four Georgians" who once scratched for gold at its foot is still there, reminding us that we are not so far removed from our wild roots.

From a distance and from close up, Mount Helena presents a harmony of historic landmark and handsome landscape befitting Big Sky Country. Our appreciation of and respect for the mountain are tributes to its endurance and the regard of good neighbors.

Mount Helena was dedicated a Natural Park by the City of Helena, to ensure that the park's natural character is maintained in perpetuity for the visual and recreational enjoyment of future generations. The intent of such dedication is to preserve, protect, and maintain the park's natural, scenic, historic, educational, and recreational resources for the enjoyment of all present and future citizens of Helena.

This friendly mountain is a park, to be sure, but it is not a land set apart. It is a place central and integral to Helena, made so by countless footsteps rather than by legal deed.

Those of us who contributed to this book could no more guide those footsteps than we could create the intimacy and exhilaration that Mount Helena offers. This explorer's manual is merely an introduction to a place that is both teacher and classroom. We all can return there time after time and see things anew. May you add many new chapters of your own.

Mount Helena, April 1996. Wayne Phillips photo.

MOUNT HELENA: A HISTORY OF IMPROVEMENT

by Erin Turner

When the April 17, 1900, edition of the *Helena Semi-Weekly Independent* hit the newsstands, Helenans were as much surprised to learn that their mountain, long called Mount Helena, had originally been given another name, as they were saddened to learn that one of Helena's beloved first residents had passed away. Known to all as "Uncle Johnny," John Cowan —one of the "Four Georgians" —had recently died at his home in Georgia, and the Helena folks were just getting wind of it.

The newspaper ran a touching account of Uncle Johnny's life, provided by one-time Cowan companion and current county treasurer William L. Steele. Steele recalled that in 1864, just after the discovery of gold in the gulch, he was sitting in Uncle Johnny's cabin with Cowan's nephews. The boys decided at that time that Mount Helena, Mount Ascension, and the ridge between them should be named for the first discoverers of Last Chance Gulch. At the time of Uncle Johnny's death, Steele expressed his disappointment that Mount Helena's other name—Mount Cowan—had long since been forgotten.

It was perhaps fortunate for the mountain, however, that it was not christened after a beloved first citizen, but rather endowed with the name of the city that grew in its shadow. By proximity, by dependency, and by name, Helenans have been linked to Mount Helena since Uncle Johnny's first gold strike in Last Chance Gulch. The mountain dominates our landscape, and although we have been neglectful of its care at times, Helenans feel a great love for and responsibility toward our mountain.

Indian camp about 1874, a treeless Mount Helena in the distance.
Courtesy Montana Historical Society, Helena.

EARLY ARRIVALS

The first people to see Mount Helena were probably hunters who began emigrating over the Bering Land Bridge between present-day Siberia and Alaska more than 25,000 years ago. Over thousands and thousands of years, more and more people settled in the eastern shadow of the Rocky Mountains because it was relatively ice free and many game species ranged here. The Scratchgravel Hills near Helena have yielded archaeological evidence pointing to these early hunters and their prey—bison, elk, bears, mastodons, antelope, wolves, and large cats.

As the climate grew drier and warmer and the prey grew smaller, these early peoples adapted to the changes, remaining in the area. The high ground surrounding the valley was apparently always a popular camp spot; Mount Helena itself may have been a meeting site or used for communication because of its prominence in the landscape. Perhaps early peoples were even familiar with the cave now called Devil's Kitchen. We can only make educated guesses. Mount Helena lies within territories which were historically occupied by both Salish and Blackfeet tribes. Although the mountain likely witnessed more than 20,000 years of human activity before any English-speaking peoples arrived, any traces of early peoples on Mount Helena prior to the 1860s have been erased by what has taken place since then.

The first English-speakers to see Mount Helena were probably explorers, miners, and frontiersmen. Explorers Meriwether Lewis and William Clark may have observed the mountain in the distance as they passed on their way to the Pacific Ocean in 1805. Other explorers, hunters, and trappers were almost certainly in the area in the mid-1800s. The only written record we have of any activity on Mount Helena prior to the gold strike in 1864 came from an old frontiersman identified only as J. A. O., who told his amazing story to a Helena newspaper in 1889.

It seems that, in 1863, J. A. O. and a companion followed a band of elk up Mount Helena hoping to procure some tasty dinner, when they came upon Devil's Kitchen. Intense curiosity prompted them to abandon their elk hunt and explore the cave. Much to their surprise, in the rear of the cave they came upon a cache of food and coffee and a note:

> Dear Tom: me and the boys have gone to bannack
> we have leaft some flour and coffee and bacon, the sugar
> got wet and is spilt. the indians stole the 2 pak horses.

J. A. O. told the newspaper that he and his partner replaced the note and the food and went on—perhaps hoping to catch up with dinner. Apparently, as they traveled north from the mountain, they ran into "Indian troubles" of their own, and they were forced to head back to the mountain. Once there, having killed one of the elusive elk, they returned to the cave and feasted on the fresh meat and the supplies left there.

One can only wonder at J. A. O.'s reticence in not having told this fascinating story before 1889, but perhaps late in life he felt pangs of guilt for having deprived the unknown Tom of his rations, and unburdened himself to the newspaper to absolve his "great sin." Even though this highly apocryphal account came thirty years after the event it describes, it is the only record of an exploration of the mountain prior to the discovery of gold in the gulch.

THE CAMP IN THE GULCH

Whether or not J. A. O.'s story is true, 1863 would have been the last year of relative solitude for Mount Helena. In 1864, the four prospectors later called the "Four Georgians" decided to try their luck panning for gold on a creek they called Last Chance at the base of the mountain. They struck it rich, and gold mining operations that developed in the gulch would eventually yield more than $30,000,000.

Practically overnight, a booming mining camp grew up around the base of the mountain—and that mining camp needed logs. Mount Helena's trees were harvested wholesale to provide timber for the mining operations, for shelter, and for fuel. As the population and number of buildings crowded into the gulch grew, the demands on the mountain increased.

By the 1870s most of the mountain's timber had been removed in the face of rapid urban development. Only a few stands of trees remained, in the most rugged, hard-to-reach spots. The population of the new town of Helena had grown substantially in the short period since the discovery of

Early Lawrence Street with Mount Helena in the distance.
Courtesy Montana Historical Society, Helena.

gold. By 1870 it had 5,000 residents, mostly miners, and the merchants who came to make money by selling various goods and services to the miners.

Mount Helena was now denuded of timber, but after several devastating fires in the gulch destroyed many of the wooden buildings, the growing population called upon the mountain for different building materials. Both limestone and quartzite were quarried on the mountain in the 1870s and 1880s. The limestone was used mostly for mortar and was baked in the kilns on the southeast side of the mountain. The quartzite was used for building stones. The mountain helped to build the city. It would be many years before the city would try to return the favor to the mountain.

In addition to taking building materials from the mountain, Helenans became adept in using the land for other civic purposes. For example, in the 1860s, water coming into the gulch through placer-mining operations was considered unfit to drink. In 1865, a canal was built to bring water from Tenmile Creek, but the burgeoning population needed another supply. One solution was to build a reservoir for the city on Mount Helena. The No. 1 Woolston Reservoir —now a permanent feature—was built in 1888 on the site of a former limestone quarry to help supply the city with fresh, clean water. It was joined by a second city reservoir in the 1930s.

On one notable Fourth of July, 1888, the mountain was used for target practice— celebratory artillery fire was aimed at it from below. The Helena Light Artillery shot "12 pounders" at the mountain in a practice/celebration shoot.

More mining attempts were made after the initial gold strike. A copper mining company was interested in the mountain near the turn of the century. In 1901, the Mount Helena Tunnel & Mining Company was formed by Thomas Cruse, Ed Zimmerman, and others to start a mine on the mountain. Either their work or work to produce lime resulted in the deep shafts for which the Prospect Shafts Trail is named. The Mount Helena Tunnel and Mining Company folded shortly after it was formed when the promised copper deposits failed to materialize.

In spite of its pitted surface and lack of shade, the mountain was also used for recreational pursuits during this early period. Mount Helena was the site of many civic celebrations. On one notable Fourth of July, 1888, the mountain was used for target practice—celebratory artillery fire was aimed at it from below. The Helena Light Artillery shot "12 pounders" at the mountain in a practice/celebration shoot. A local newspaper reported, "Full loaded shells were numerously exploded, and the scarred face of the mountain told the effect of every shot." As if shooting cannonballs at the side of the mountain were not enough of a celebration, when Helena won the fight for the capital in 1894, a huge bonfire, fueled by anything that would burn, was built on the mountain to celebrate the victory over Anaconda. The fire could be seen all over the valley.

In the 1870s and 1880s Helena's residents frequently took to the mountain on foot for their romps. The *Helena Herald* gave a report of a picnic in 1875, where:

> A party of ladies and gentlemen numbering some 15 or 20, made the ascent of Mount Helena on Saturday, and on the summit of that stupendous hill, had a picnic—a genuine frolic. Some of the excursionists made the ascent on foot, and others on horseback. We know of one young lady at least who made the round trip on foot. . . . At 5 p.m. the picknickers partook of a lunch which is represented to have been prepared in a style commensurate with the jolly occasion, and capable of satiating the keen appetites that were engendered by ascending this precipitous mount—2,200 feet above the city. Two kegs of Nick Kessler's XXX lager beer, and a dozen bottles of Heisdick's best served as pacifiers. After lunch—later in the evening—when night had drawn her sable curtain down—there were bonfires and illuminations, and a brilliant display of pyrotechnics which were generally observed in Helena, and greatly admired.

Almost a decade later, in 1882, the *Helena Herald* was a great proponent of pedestrian excursions to the top of Mount Helena—especially at sunrise or sunset when, it said, "visitors would witness a greater revelation of beauty than can be found in all the art galleries on both continents. . . . Do not deny yourself the health and pleasure of the moderate, but delightful walk. Go all, and go often."

One can imagine, however, that these excursions were not undertaken without a certain amount of effort and risk. Much to the consternation of

The Circle Library Group picnics on Mount Helena, 1902.
Courtesy Montana Historical Society, Helena.

many citizens, domestic animals were allowed to graze freely on the mountain. By 1899 large numbers of goats roamed about on Mount Helena, and cows and horses were allowed this liberty as well. Not only were these animals damaging the vegetation of the mountainside, they were a great nuisance to the recreationists. Members of the Helena Bicycle Club complained that the "voracious" west side cows had eaten the posts from a fence they had erected to mark a bike path. Indeed, there was much general concern about the cows roaming about the Upper West Side, "without visible means of support."

A SOCIETY FOR IMPROVEMENT

In spite of the fact that Mount Helena was bald, pitted, scarred, and overrun by maverick cows and goats, people still held it in their affections. It wasn't until the 1890s, however, that Helena residents began to say enough was enough—they had seen too much rampant abuse of their city's surrounding landscape. Before the end of the nineteenth century, even the most progressive and open-minded of Helena's citizens would have had no reason to believe that it was inappropriate to use the mountain in any other way than it had been. However, nationwide stirrings of the conservation movement in the 1890s would have reached Helena and would probably have helped encourage its citizens to preserve the mountain as a park.

Other motivating forces may have been at work as well. By 1890, the population of Helena had grown to almost 14,000. The city had been the territorial capital since 1875 and in 1894, five years after Montana became a state, it would win the fight for the right to be the state capital over Anaconda. In addition, Helena was said to have more millionaires per capita than any other city in the United States. Mount Helena was becoming the backyard for many of the city's prominent residents, who were building their mansions on the lower slopes of the mountain above the gulch. The mountain—scruffy as it was—was a rather unbecoming backdrop for the up-and-coming city. All of these factors, as well as the frustration of the bicycle club and other recreationists, probably encouraged the residents of Helena to do something to improve the mountain's landscape.

The first official event designed to help better Mount Helena was an Arbor Day celebration held in 1899. Groups of schoolchildren ascended the mountain, each child carrying a pine seedling and an orange. As they made their way up the mountain to the area where the young trees were to be planted, they were serenaded by Helena violinist Fred Kuphal. Kuphal was a native of Germany who came to Helena with his parents in 1882 when he was two years old. He began playing the violin at a very young age, and eventually returned to Germany to study music. After completing his education, he returned to Helena to direct orchestras at the Ming Opera House and Helena High School. In 1913, he and his wife moved to Los Angeles, where he played with the Los Angeles Philharmonic and became their personnel manager and librarian. He retired at age 80.

In 1966, sixty-seven years after Kuphal serenaded the Arbor Day planting, the City of Helena named the stand of remaining trees the Fred Kuphal Grove in his honor. The campaign to name the grove for Kuphal was spearheaded by Frieda Fligelman of Helena, one of the schoolchildren who participated in the planting. Although no plaque or memorial stands to mark its place, the grove of trees still stands on the mountain.

After that first Arbor Day planting, further improvements on the mountain were taken on by a group called the Helena Improvement Society.

—A—
MOVEABLE HOUSE

The Helena Independent,
circa 1890

Freaks of the Chinook with a
mountain abode near Helena.

Perched on a giddy height half way up the northern slope of Mount Helena stands, or rather did stand a few days ago, the house of Mr. Langford, Col. Broadwater's private secretary, who last year took up a forty acre tract of mountain land in that locality and built a house upon it. The house, erected upon a lofty eminence several hundred feet higher than the city, appeared to curious spectators in the valley below like a Swiss cottage hung in mid-air, or some lonely resort near the snow line on the ascent to Mount Blanc. The hillside domicile was built, the first story of stone and the second of wood, and safely withstood the winds of summer and the frosts of early winter. But when the chinook crept over the crest of Mount Helena a few days ago, the mountain tenement trembled to its foundation at each successive gust, until finally an extraordinarily fierce volley of the south wind's artillery lifted the frame portion gently off the stone substructure and carried it bodily up the mountain and, towards town, where it alighted right side up on a level patch of ground. The next morning people living at the base of the mountain were surprised to see a new frame house on a spot that the day before was vacant, but the phenomenon was quickly explained by a glance at the dismantled stone work of the Langford house, which loomed up minus its second story. Old Chinook, however, wanted to have some more fun, so on Friday night he sent some of his gentle zephyrs after the house again, and this time they picked it up bodily as before and carried it down the mountain towards town, separating it still farther from its original site and again astonishing West Side residents by showing them another new house built in a single night. At last accounts the structure still held together and stood rightside up, looking like a low frame house built upon the bleak hill-side. What the Chinook did with it yesterday has not been learned, but when last heard from John Heldt, who lives at the base of Mount Helena and seemingly in the path of the wandering edifice, was threatening to lasso the erratic structure and make a barn of it, providing the chinook would be accommodating enough to deposit it in his back yard. ♦

The society was founded in 1898 with thirty charter members, and was perhaps the most vital source of support behind the drive to clean up the city and Mount Helena. They funded their good works through membership dues of $1 per year or $25 for a lifetime, as well as through grand balls and concerts. Most of their early efforts revolved around cleaning up the city itself. The society was devoted to planting trees along major thoroughfares, particularly on Sixth Avenue between the new capitol and the gulch. Its members were also responsible for landscaping at the city's schools. It wasn't until 1902, however, that they would turn their attention to the mountain with the idea of creating a city park.

Early in the 1890s, the suggestion had been made—probably by John S. M. Neil, the publisher of the *Helena Independent* and a great advocate of improving the mountain—that something should be done about Mount Helena. The idea circulated for a time that the city should create a Grand Pleasure Resort on the mountain, complete with botanical gardens, fountains, and a "gravity railroad" making frequent trips to the top. The idea was brought up frequently, with embellishments, for several years, and resurfaced when Helena was making its case to be the state capital, but never came to fruition. In 1902, when the Helena Improvement Society was able to concentrate its efforts on the mountain, the current plan was to create a forest park on Mount Helena.

The increased effort on the part of the society came partially from a number of small fires that were started on the mountain between 1898 and 1901, considered to be arson fires. The society offered the enormous sum of $25 (or perhaps they would have substituted a lifetime membership), for information leading to the arrest of the perpetrators of the heinous crimes. This probably scared the boys who had been starting the fires away from the mountain, but a metaphorical fire was lit under the Helena Improvement Society. Its plans to improve the mountain were put into motion.

The group sent a delegation to Washington, D.C., to convince Congress to declare the park a national preserve. When Congress failed to make the declaration, a new plan was developed. Rather than build a grand pleasure resort, the Helena Improvement Society would erect a simple pavilion on the summit of the mountain, reached by a path with a gentle grade. By 1903, the plan was given the go ahead, and in June the first

Russell Aubrey Shaw and children sit in the pavilion atop Mount Helena, 1913.
Courtesy Montana Historical Society, Helena.

survey for the path was completed. In August, the trail (now inaccurately called the 1906 Trail) was complete, and benches had been installed every 100 feet along the path. From the summit after a now easy climb, the whole valley was visible in panorama below. The path was not trouble-free, however. Shortly after it was completed and much to the dismay of the Society, local businesses placed advertisements on the benches, but those were easily wiped away with a coat of paint.

That winter, the Improvement Society, impressed with its recent success, tried to further protect the mountain by posting notices that anyone caught removing Christmas trees from the mountain would be arrested. In addition, its plans for the pavilion on the summit were completed, and in June 1904 the building began. Before a crowd of two hundred people on July 4, 1904, the shelter house was dedicated. Two weeks later, it would be damaged slightly when it was struck by lightning. It was removed in the 1930s.

Shortly after the dedication of the pavilion, the drive to reforest the land began. To do so, the society first had to gain ownership of the mountain so that they could declare it a city park.

When the Helena Improvement Society and the City of Helena announced their plans to turn the mountain into a park and reforest it, the city received a patent on 160 acres on the mountain. After that achievement, the drive to acquire more land was on. The Helena Improvement Society began encouraging all citizens of Helena who owned property on the mountain to donate it to the city. Shortly after the first bit of land was acquired, a Mr. and Mrs. Biggs donated 120 acres to the effort. The *Helena Independent* ran with the news and began to report on the prospective land deals. By May 1905, the newspaper announced that the park would soon have 700 acres of land; by July it was reporting 800 acres; and by the beginning of September the prospective acreage had reached a staggering 1,000 acres.

… its plans for the pavilion on the summit were completed, and in June 1904 the building began. Before a crowd of two hundred people on July 4, 1904, the shelter house was dedicated.

In December, the Helena Improvement Society had sufficient faith in its ability to procure the land that they announced on warning signs to Christmas tree hunters that the Mount Helena Forest Park was now owned by the city. In January 1906, however, it was revealed that the city had actually acquired only 360 acres on the mountain. Undaunted, the society went on to discuss plans for reforesting Mount Helena.

Earlier, in 1905, the Helena Improvement Society had begun consulting with U.S. Chief Forester Gifford Pinchot and his assistant, E. A. Sterling, about reforesting the mountain. Originally, the group planned on planting 500,000 trees (if the *Helena Independent's* math can be trusted), but in August 1905 that number was reduced to 50,000 with additional plantings to take place over the next ten years.

It was becoming more and more obvious how important the mountain was to the citizens of Helena. The *Helena Independent* took a break from its reports on the planting in its August 11, 1905, issue to tell about Helena resident Gilbert Benedict, more than 70 years old, who climbed the mountain every day with a shovel to remove rocks from the footpath. Not to be outdone in civic duty by this near octogenarian, that September the Reverend S. S. Healy led a group of boys to a nearby forest to begin collecting seed cones to reforest the mountain. In late 1905, Pinchot approved the planting of seedlings from a Forest Service nursery. The plan was announced in February 1906: As an experiment, the Forest Service would provide more than 25,000 trees for planting on the mountain.

Later that year, 10,000 yellow (ponderosa) pine and 20,000 Douglas-fir from the Forest Service were planted on Mount Helena using day laborers from town at a total cost of $311.30. The results of this first planting were not encouraging. In August 1906, Jay Bond, a forest assistant, was compelled to report that none of the trees from the first planting had survived. Undaunted, the Forest Service tried planting seedlings again that fall, and this time the results were much more favorable. The following April, an assessment was made revealing that 92 percent of the Douglas-fir and 60 percent of the yellow pine had survived.

A HILL WITH A FENCE AROUND IT

Over the next sixty years, land was added to the park and trees were planted there, but the Helena Improvement Society turned its interest to other projects and then disbanded. As early as 1909 the *Helena Independent* lamented,

> We have a forest park on Mount Helena which is neglected, and should have attention. There is work for the Helena Improvement Society and plenty of it. That worthy institution should be rehabilitated and made an agency for good. It should be revived from the apparent lethargy in which the organization has fallen.

In 1911, a Helena citizen mourned the demise of the Improvement Society. "A glimpse of Mount Helena recalls wistful memories of six years ago when the Helena Improvement Society took on new and vigorous life. . . . The Helena Improvement Society is only a memory. The Mount Helena Forest Park is a hill with a fence around it."

The world and Helena were in great turmoil during the first part of the twentieth century. First World War I, then the Great Depression, then

Dodge Touring Car atop Mount Helena, 1916.
Courtesy Montana Historical Society, Helena

the great 1935 earthquakes and fire in Helena, and then World War II drew the interests of Helenans away from improving their city park. It wasn't totally ignored, however. Though much less was done to improve Mount Helena, it was still used regularly for recreation and other purposes. Although there were foot races up the mountain as early as 1913, in 1916, the first "official" race up Mount Helena was run. In 1924 the tradition of painting the "H" on the side of the mountain was started by Helena High School seniors.

During World War II, the mountain was used as a training ground for an elite special force of Canadian and American troops. These troops were to be a commando force, trained in parachuting, skiing, rock climbing, and other combat tactics. Before the men were even fully trained on Mount Helena and at nearby Fort Harrison, they were called to southern France and Italy to fight. It was said that they were superbly trained nonetheless, and that it was they who "won the war in Europe." The rumors of their training and skills caused so much terror among German troops that the German commanders circulated a memo stating "You are fighting an elite Canadian-American force. They are treacherous, unmerciful, and clever.

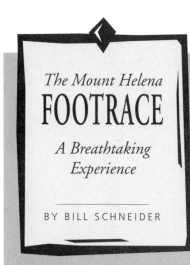

The Mount Helena
FOOTRACE
A Breathtaking Experience

BY BILL SCHNEIDER

Long before running for fitness became popular, people have been racing to the top of Mount Helena. In fact, the first race up the mountain was held in 1916.

In the mid-1970s, local runners found historical articles from the *Helena Daily Independent* about this first race. Vic Norman, a famous long-distance runner from "the coast" was in town and favored to win. But a local amateur runner named Ben Burgess (who had to run his milk delivery route each morning to keep up with his horse) triumphed over Norman. Harvey "Speed" Yates of Helena finished second, also defeating the favorite from the coast.

On September 20, 1975, local runners re-enacted the 1916 run, with 108 runners participating. Bill Lannan of Helena won the 1975 race with a time of 35 minutes, 9 seconds. Since then the race has been run every September. In 1975, race organizers established the Ben Burgess Memorial Award, and each year the overall male and female winners are inscribed on the plaque, which is on display in the Helena Area Chamber of Commerce office in downtown Helena.

The race course now starts on the downtown pedestrian mall in front of the New York Block and goes south down the mall to the Neighborhood Center, where runners turn right. Passing through historic Reeder's Alley, then up Adams Street, they take the Prairie Trail around the backside of the mountain and run up the feared Hogback to the summit. After taking a deep breath or two, they run down the 1906 Trail and finish at the Neighborhood Center. It is a 5.3-mile course with a 1,368-foot elevation gain.

Although the exact course of the 1916 run is unknown, Burgess ran to the top of the mountain and back in 30 minutes, 58 seconds, more than 5 minutes faster than anyone has run the modern-day event. The fastest times on the new course to date are 36 minutes, 10 seconds for men (Patrick Judge, 1995) and 46 minutes, 26 seconds for women (Cheryl Johnson, 1981). ♦

... in 1916, the "first" race up Mount Helena was run. In 1924, the tradition of painting the "H" on the side of the mountain was started by Helena High School seniors.

You cannot afford to relax. The first soldier or group of soldiers capturing one of these men will be given a ten-day furlough."

THE MOUNTAIN TODAY

While the commandos were training on the mountain, domestic animals were still allowed to graze there—although presumably they were not used for target practice. By the 1970s, however, grazing had become overgrazing, motorcycles and 4-wheel drive vehicles were deeply scarring the hillsides, the mountain was strewn with litter, and a cluster of communication antennae had taken up residence atop the mountain. To combat these problems, a group called the Save Mount Helena Committee was formed. In 1972 they presented these problems to the city commission, resulting in the cancellation of the horse grazing lease, installation of signs, and increased law enforcement of the existing city ordinance prohibiting motor vehicles in city parks.

The Save Mount Helena Committee was successful in getting additional improvements to the park funded through the Model City Program in the mid-1970s. With these funds, the city surveyed and marked the boundary of the park, a task that had been long neglected. Barriers to control motor vehicle access and a new parking facility at the end of Adams Street were constructed. Picnic tables and trash disposal facilities were installed. The effort to control the erosion in the park became a community project. Many volunteers enthusiastically contributed to the effort to heal the scars from cross-country vehicles. They built drainage ditches, seeded, and mulched.

The Youth Conservation Corps was recruited to work on the park, as well. They spent several summers cleaning up garbage, marking the park boundary, closing off mine shafts, installing signs, and constructing trails.

Also in the 1970s, the Bureau of Land Management "sold" the city of Helena another 151 acres of land on the mountain, returning the check the next year. This increased the size of the park to 620 acres. Additionally, a sculpture of Mount Helena (which received mixed reviews) was installed

Planting trees in the 1970s. Wayne Phillips photo.

on the city's new walking mall, and the Mount Helena Run was revived. Most important, perhaps, was the establishment of the seven new official trails, which probably encouraged more use of the mountain as a park and also helped protect it. The seven trails added were the Prairie, Hogback, Prospects Shafts, Back Side, East Side, West End, and North Access routes. The 1906 Trail, built by the Helena Improvement Society in 1903, was added to the National Recreational Trail System in 1979, in combination with the 4.5 miles of Forest Service trail that make up the "Ridge Trail." Shortly thereafter, its work apparently done, the Save Mount Helena Committee disappeared from public record.

In the 1980s, in response to the placing of an emergency signal tower on the mountain, the Friends of Mount Helena stepped in to save the mountain from further development, and then faded from sight. In the 1990s, the Mount Helena Trail User's Group continues to be visible. Two more trails were added to the mountain in 1995, the Panhandle and Quartzite trails, and a kiosk with a map was installed at the Adams Street parking lot. Recently, local businesses have "adopted" the mountain, volunteering for clean-up duty and noxious weed removal.

17

Shortly after the founding of the Friends of Mount Helena in 1985, the *Independent Record*, continuing its tradition of interest in the park, asked, "Will Helenans again nearly forget the mountain's existence?" It seems that we will not, although our commitment may falter temporarily. Clearly, the mountain is a part of our city as much as the Saint Helena Cathedral or the Capitol. It is Mount Helena, not Mount Cowan, after all —our mountain and our shared responsibility.

Editors' Note: Land acquisition on Mount Helena has continued into the last decade of the twentieth century. In 1997, two additional parcels of land were added to the park, and more will likely follow. Additionally, Mount Helena has recently found a place on the National Register of Historic Places. It is now recognized as a Historic District.

MAMMALS, REPTILES, AND AMPHIBIANS

by Gayle Joslin

Mount Helena—symbol of Montana's capital city, community park, and our connection to the wild. Every day, Mount Helena influences us and is influenced by the human culture associated with its ecology. It reminds us that we are not far removed from our wild roots if we open ourselves to nature's subtle messages and learn to read the signs our wild neighbors leave. The old mountain also quietly beckons to us, teasing us with the opportunity of reconnecting with nature. This connection can be made casually, on a 20-minute stroll, or more profoundly, with an extended trek into the home of deer, elk, cougar, coyote, and bear, and the former home of wolf who may someday be seen passing over the snow in the January moonlight after many years' absence.

Your courteous sensitivity in the home of these animals, and to the animals themselves, is what makes Mount Helena so special to the wild inhabitants and the human visitors. No matter what kind of wildlife opportunity presents itself to you on the mountain, please remain a safe and respectful distance away. Do not attempt to pursue, catch, or feed wild animals. And, of course, leave habitat as you find it. The object of wildlife watching is never to see how close you can get, but rather to see how subtly you can experience a wild creatures' presence before passing on your way.

PART OF A LARGER WHOLE
Wild animals use Mount Helena extensively, just as they use the big sweep of country that stretches to the south and west. The mountain park is the

north end of a long ridge that connects our well-developed human community to wild communities inhabiting Black Mountain, Red Mountain, Electric Peak, Thunderbolt Mountain, the Three Brothers, and other wild places along the Continental Divide. Follow the geography far enough south, and eventually you'll find civilization again—the Mining City of Butte. U.S. Highway 12 curves off MacDonald Pass from the west and swings east into Helena, serving as the boundary for Mount Helena on the west and north. Open, rolling foothills extend westward toward Mullan Pass from the base of the mountain. Together with the highway, this open country creates somewhat of a barrier to wildlife movements. The northwest edge of the timbered mountain nevertheless is consistently used by emigrating wildlife as a stepping-off point for their movements west and north.

... bushy-tailed woodrats have built an extensive, messy abode of sticks, bones, and shiny bits of trash. Like the humans living below the mountain slopes, these critters are collectors of stuff.

In addition to the big, exciting creatures that seasonally pass through our park, many animals live here full time. For example, under a north-facing limestone cliff overlooking the city, bushy-tailed woodrats (packrats) have built an extensive, messy abode of sticks, bones, and shiny bits of trash. Like the humans living below the mountain slopes, these critters are collectors of stuff. And like some of the first human residents of the gulch, these "packrats" stuck their outhouse out back. Below the nest a large, black, shiny mass clings to the cliff face—a natural latrine. Fecal material clinging to the vertical rock face is dissolved and restructured by highly acidic packrat urine, creating a hard crust that now decorates the limestone cliffs. Over the years, one such "decoration" on the mountain has grown as big as a highway billboard. The size of this and other deposits attests to the quality of the packrat habitat on the mountain. It has taken many generations of rodent families living in the same place to create a manure pile of this proportion.

These woodrat dwellings are not to be confused with other stick nests on the ledges of the mountain's limestone escarpments. In past years raptors (birds of prey) have inhabited nests on Mount Helena's north rim. Prairie falcons were the primary nesters here. However, increased use of the mountain seems to have rendered the cliffs less attractive to these birds—another reminder to treat wildlife with respect, and to appreciate them from a distance.

Unless you are a crepuscular hiker—one who likes to go out at dawn or dusk—your only exposure to the several species of bats that live in the mountain's tunnel-riddled cliffs will be the white traces of guano (bat feces) that streak the vertical rocks. At least three species of bats are likely residents in the park. These lovers of the night emerge from their hidden limestone caverns to feed almost exclusively on insects. It is probable that this nocturnal bug-control service extends through a substantial portion of the town below.

Critters as diverse as salamanders, gopher snakes, and golden-mantled ground squirrels inhabit the mountain park as well. Two species of amphibians (a salamander and a toad), six reptiles (all snakes), and more than three dozen mammals may use Mount Helena and the ridge running south from the park at some time of the year. The fact that some animals only use the park seasonally does not diminish the land's importance. Many

The black mass in this photo of the rock face of Mount Helena is actually a solidified mound of packrat scat. Gayle Joslin photo.

animals require an extended habitat, and the mountain's grass and sage slopes and timber meet seasonally critical habitat needs. Mount Helena is a crucial link in a land base used by animal communities that occupy a much larger area. This demonstrates that the mountain, like the capital city itself, has an importance and an influence capable of reaching well beyond the dimensions of its physical geography.

SIGNS OF LIFE

If you are a casual hiker, you probably won't observe much of the wildlife that lives on the mountain. However, if you exercise a keen eye you will be able to tell where these animals have been by noticing their calling cards—tracks, scat or feces, scrapes, rubs, gnaw marks, nibbled shrubs, and even excavation tailings.

... approached by an attacker or curious contemporary, the porky is not so slow after all.

Tailings—mysterious tubes of dirt lying quite precisely atop the ground—are one of the more interesting animal "signs." These "core samples" of soil are usually found in mountain meadows. They are the result of the subnivean (under-snow) roto-tilling excavations of pocket gophers in winter. These particular gophers are subterranean pocket-faced rodents that rarely show themselves. They tunnel under the turf, clipping off roots and other food, then stuffing it into external pouches on their cheeks. The snow holds the cylinders of gopher-moved duff and dirt semi-vertically until a spring thaw gently places them on the ground's surface.

Attentive park visitors can find other signs of wild neighbors. "Rubs" are marks caused by male ungulates (hoofed mammals) as they rub off the blood-filled, bone-producing velvet of their antlers. Once a deer, elk, or moose completes its antler-growing cycle, the velvet dries up and is scraped off the new head ornaments by active rubbing on a sapling tree.

Tree trunks may bear a variety of other telltale marks announcing animals' presence. Bears will use tree trunks in an attempt to display their size and claim their turf, reaching high to leave claw imprints in the bark. They usually do this by standing on their hind legs and scratching the tree with their forepaws. The bark eventually heals in long, rounded scars.

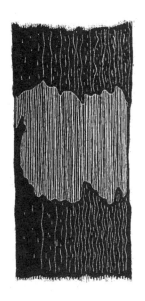

ANIMAL CALLING CARDS

Porcupine-gnawed tree.

Excavation tailings.

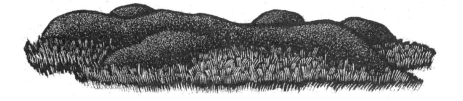

Mountain lion scrape and scat.

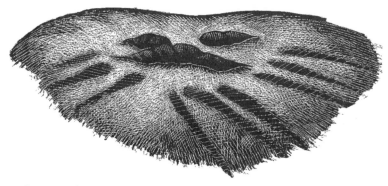

Illustrations by Peter Grosshauser

If tree bark has been removed in a glowing, golden patch, it is usually a sign that a porcupine has dined on the inner cambium, just under the bark's surface. These "quill-pigs" seem to favor conifers. Unless the porcupine feeds all the way around the tree trunk, girdling its food source, the tree usually survives. In time the "wound" will heal, rounding on the edges and at times resembling the old blaze marks that humans made along forest trails.

Porcupines are one of the largest members of the rodent family. Although slow and awkward, they have formidable quill defenses. When approached by an attacker or curious contemporary, the porky is not so slow after all. It can spin around quite quickly, but cannot throw quills. A porcupine must make physical contact with its target—for this it uses its tail. If an attacker can successfully flip the porky onto its back, its bare, vulnerable stomach is exposed. This technique has been mastered by the porcupine's arch-enemy, the fisher. The fisher also has the rare capacity to digest and pass porcupine quills through its digestive system. Fishers do not occur on Mount Helena, but they may live in the roadless country to the south. The porcupine's presence here is certain, though, and is another good reason to keep your dog under control in the forest. Pulling quills from a pet's mouth and tongue is a nasty business.

Smaller rodent cousins to the porcupine are the ubiquitous and very busy chipmunks and red squirrels. These are opportunistic hunters, searching for seeds, nuts, and insects. Squirrels will methodically hunt for bird nests in search of nestlings to prey upon. Action-packed arboreal battles can be observed when a pair of robins defend their nest against a marauding squirrel.

THE CRITICAL SEASON

Squirrels are of necessity an enterprising group, since they actively endure the winters here. To do so they build substantial middens (caches) of conifer cones, storing them in hollow trees, under logs, or around the gnarled, protruding roots of a large pine, fir, or spruce. A squirrel midden might contain enough cones to fill a good-sized doghouse. By contrast, the squirrel's smaller chipmunk cousins will snugly hibernate the winter away in a cozy nest.

On particularly snowy days, elk can sometimes be seen on the northeast slope of the mountain from the complex surrounding the State Capitol.

More reliably, however, they are known to use the west slopes of Mount Helena. The quiet, snowy, short days of deep winter can be formidable for elk. For them, it is a time when their survival is at stake—winter is the time known as "critical" to biologists. Mount Helena and the ridge to its south are vitally important winter range for about two hundred elk. They seek the open grassy slopes, the nutritious sage and bitterbrush,

... deep winter can be formidable for elk. ... it is a time when their survival is at stake—winter is the time known as "critical" to biologists.

and the cover provided by Douglas-fir, ponderosa, and lodgepole thickets. When night temperatures plummet, the coniferous forest provides thermal protection by capturing and slowing heat loss from animals, vegetation, and the earth to the sky. Big trees also hold some daylight heat in their massive trunks, and groves of them are favored bedding spots for wildlife.

Somewhat similar to the central heating or cooling system of your home, these taller, multi-layered levels of forest vegetation on the mountain are important in all seasons, providing heat control for animals in the form of shade in summer and preventing heat loss in winter. The ways in which animals use the various parts of the mountain are how they control their comfort level. Large animals such as deer, elk, moose, and lion require substantial areas of landscape to meet their comfort, security, and nutritional needs. The total area occupied through the seasons is known as the home range. During spring, summer, and fall, these animals range south into the Black Mountain and Red Mountain country. Their survival and health, however, usually depend on the drier, sunnier Mount Helena ridge where they patiently endure the winter. This is the season when it is especially important to view them from a distance. During tough winters, they have no fat or enegry to spare, and added stress could be a burden, making the difference between being a winter-kill statistic, or a doe that lives to see spring and is capable of bringing new life to our mountains.

While elk are primarily grazers, eating grass and low-growing forbs, mule deer and moose are browsers, feeding on a variety of shrubs. Bears relish the succulent vegetation of seeps, springs, bogs, and creek bottoms, but they also dig for the starchy tubers and roots of plants such as claytonia and wild carrot, which grow on dry slopes and ridgetops. Bears are

... Mount Helena holds good news for those who know how to read what animals write in the dust and snow among its trees.

omnivorous, feeding not only upon vegetation but also on carrion, insects, and occasionally live critters such as ground squirrels or fawns. Mountain lions, on the other hand, are almost exclusively carnivorous—and they prefer their meat relatively fresh. Once a lion has made a kill and consumed what it wants for the moment, it will carefully place the carcass in a shady place and cover it with needles and duff for storage until the next meal. A family of lions may consume all but the hooves of a big-game animal. Lions will not generally leave portions of a carcass behind unless the weather is warm and decay has begun.

PREDATOR AND PREY

Although finding wolves on Mount Helena would be a rare event, finding mountain lions there is not. But you probably won't see a lion—even seasoned hunters who have spent years wandering the mountains may never spot one of the big cats. Lions are regular visitors here, and winter hikers may find their tracks and territorial scrapes of urine, dirt, and conifer duff left as the tawny beasts search the mountain for deer, stray pets, and other prey.

As mountain lion populations expand, young cats are forced to find and establish territories of their own. Confrontations with humans can occur as these hungry juveniles drift into the edges of our communities. Hikers should behave in a proper manner if they encounter a lion—stand your ground, do not run or turn your back on the lion, try to look bigger by raising your arms or spreading your coat, pick up children and small pets, and talk in a low, even voice.

Moose are only occasional visitors to Mount Helena Park, but they regularly traverse the ridge between Grizzly Gulch on the east and Tenmile Creek on the west. Mule deer are year-long inhabitants of the mountain. Identify them by their large ears, black-tipped tail, and bounding gait (called "stotting"). White-tailed deer live around the edges of the mountain, particularly along Tenmile Creek and in Grizzly, Nelson, and Colorado gulches. They tend to prefer riparian (water-influenced), broad-leafed habitats of lower terrain. Whitetail characteristics include a large tail with no black tip, which they raise vertically when alarmed and wag back and forth stiffly as they flee. Whitetails do not stot as mule deer do, but run, leap, or sneak away into the brush. Both species of deer produce spotted fawns in late May or early June, but mule deer usually have only one fawn and whitetails may have twins. Mount Helena's powerfully fragrant sagebrush slopes are used by both mule deer and elk during fawning and calving. The potent fragrance of flowering sage may be too much for the sensitive nostrils of predators, masking the nearly odorless newborns. All of these large mammals are generous packets of protein on the hoof to predators, such as wolves and mountain lions.

Under cover of night, mule deer take extended bold forays into town and risk encounters with cars, dogs, and people to sample the exotic flavors of ornamental shrubs. These excursions into our neighborhoods are not the animal kingdom equivalent of a joy trip—for these deer, survival is at stake. As lawns, ornamental vegetation, fruit trees, and pavement replace

A mountain lion on a snowy slope.
Montana Department of Fish, Wildlife & Parks photo.

sage, bitterbrush, and other natural forage, the animals try to find a way to make it all work.

A CONSERVATION ETHIC

Mount Helena becomes all the more special when you consider the association between humans and wildlife that has occurred on or near the mountain. The mountain looked over this same landscape when it was Blackfeet Indian territory and wildlife had the entire Helena Valley for potential winter range. The old mountain may have taken note of explorers Meriwether Lewis and William Clark as they passed up the Missouri River to the east. Once the four men known as the "Four Georgians" found the yellow metal in the gulch at its feet, the mountain's timber was stripped for fuel and its wildlife was harvested to feed the miners—so much game was killed and sold that, for a time, there were no elk, moose, deer, or lions on its slopes. It was a dark and silent time.

... stand your ground, do not run or turn your back on the lion, try to look bigger by raising your arms or spreading your coat, pick up children and small pets, and talk in a low, even voice.

Fortunately our predecessors found a conservation ethic and a land ethic that led to the recovery of Mount Helena's wildlife. The work was in large part the achievement of conservation-minded hunters who insisted on protection, paid for law enforcement, and studied game management. With others, these conservationists protected the critical habitat necessary to sustain wildlife recovery. Today we live side by side with reasonably healthy deer, elk, lion, and other wildlife populations. This ethic, and the fruits of its success, were passed on to future generations by our predecessors who determined we could and should share this wonderful place. Mount Helena, and the wild country beyond, is a land base that supports this remarkable achievement.

Today, as throughout our history, Mount Helena holds good news for those who know how to read what animals write in the dust and snow among the trees. The mountain is part of a large tapestry—each day we learn more about how its threads are woven together. More than a lovely park with wonderful trails, trees, and open space, Mount Helena is our link to wildlife, wild country, and a conservation ethic that reaches back through generations. It is now our turn to show we can build on the conservation ethic that brought the mountain, and all the wild country it ties us to, back to life. This is what was passed on to our generation and what we will pass on to our children. It's a wild thing!

BIRDLIFE

by Dan Sullivan

One of the great advantages of the avocation of birding is that it can be done anywhere. With only binoculars and a field guide to birds, watchers can spend a few minutes or all day enjoying this pleasant and interesting diversion. In only a few minutes from any place in the city of Helena, a birder can reach the edge of the large natural area called Mount Helena. You can often see a dozen species within a few minutes, especially on a morning in late spring. For those who have a little time, a walk on the mountain's several trails, which traverse a mixture of grassland, shrub and forest habitats, offers the chance to observe a variety of bird species.

A few bird species are considered habitat generalists—that is, they can be found in a wide variety of habitats. (The American robin is a good example.) Most birds prefer to live in a particular type of habitat, however. Except during migration or dispersal, they are seldom found outside their preferred habitat. The wider the diversity of habitat types an area has, the more species of birds it will hold.

As you look at Mount Helena, what kinds of habitats do you see? No streams, lakes, or large deciduous trees are found there, so bird species that prefer those types of habitats are unlikely to occur on the mountain. Instead, Mount Helena has four basic habitats: grassland parks, deciduous shrubs, conifer forest, and rock cliffs and outcrops.

BIRDS OF THE GRASSLAND

Mount Helena's grassland parks are small when compared to the extensive grasslands found on the prairie. The mountain's most conspicuous grassland birds are the western meadowlark, vesper sparrow, and mountain bluebird.

Western meadowlark
Sturnella neglecta
Illustration by
Peter Grosshauser

The western meadowlark, *Sturnella neglecta*, is so widely distributed and so well-known by Montanans that it is designated the state bird. In fact, this meadowlark and its eastern counterpart, the eastern meadowlark, are so universally recognized by residents of the Great Plains that they are also the state birds of more than a dozen other prairie states.

Seen from the back the meadowlark is an inconspicuous brown and blends into the grassland environment when on the ground. From the front, the bird is a brilliant yellow from throat to belly, with a distinctive black "V" across the center of the breast. In flight, meadowlarks often alternate between a series of rapid wing beats and short stiff-winged glides, exposing a patch of white on each side of the tail.

Meadowlarks are often seen singing from utility poles and the tops of trees and shrubs. Frequently they are heard singing in flight. The song is composed of a series of slurry, flutelike notes—it is easily recognized and remembered after only a few repetitions.

Meadowlarks build nests on the ground, forming the grass surrounding the nest into a dome over it. If you are hiking off the trail during the nesting season you may occasionally flush a bird from a nest. Take a brief look if you like, then move on. The bird will quickly return. If you walk your dog in the park, it is important to keep the dog on a leash or close to you to prevent destruction of these nests.

The vesper sparrow, *Pooecetes gramineus*, is another grassland bird commonly found in the park. It is a small, inconspicuous bird that is mostly brown. At close range, light streaking will be seen on the breast. The most diagnostic field mark is the bird's white outer tail feathers, which are exposed in flight.

The vesper sparrow's song begins with two long slurred notes followed by two higher-pitched notes, then a series of trills. This bird is often observed singing from low-growing shrubs in grassy areas.

Mountain bluebirds, *Sialia currucoides*, are easily identified because of the sky blue color of the male. The female bluebird is mainly gray, but both her wings and tail are a dusty blue. These beautiful birds are often seen hawking from perches or hovering over open areas in search of insects.

Bluebirds, because they are cavity nesters, are not true grassland species. They are found in open woodlands or edge areas where grassland and woodland meet, such as the open grass parks found on Mount Helena. They depend on naturally occurring holes or nest sites excavated in previous years by woodpeckers. They also readily nest in birdhouses and can be found nesting in bird boxes placed in yards surrounding Mount Helena. Bluebirds commonly raise two broods a season. Sometimes the female incubates a second clutch of eggs at another nest while the male continues to care for the first nestlings on his own until they fledge. The young from the first nest may even help to provide food for the second group of nestlings.

House sparrows and starlings, both species introduced into North America from Europe, compete with bluebirds for nest sites. In many areas this has resulted in a decline of bluebird numbers. Bluebird trails, bird

Mountain bluebird
Sialia currucoides
Illustration by
Peter Grosshauser

boxes placed along roads in bluebird habitat by people interested in bluebird conservation, have increased bluebird populations in many areas.

The grassland sites of Mount Helena are less suitable for grassland bird populations with each passing year. As you walk through these areas, note the young trees and shrubby plants invading these grassy sites. Without fire or removal by other means, the grasslands of Mount Helena will disappear. Along with them will go the birds that live on these small foothill prairies.

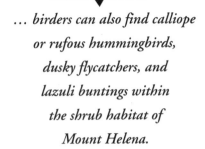

… birders can also find calliope or rufous hummingbirds, dusky flycatchers, and lazuli buntings within the shrub habitat of Mount Helena.

BIRDS OF THE DECIDUOUS SHRUBLANDS

Narrow coulees along the lower slopes of the park support a variety of shrubs, such as serviceberry, chokecherry, Rocky Mountain juniper, snowberry, and bitterbrush. These kind of plants add structural diversity and create a more complex habitat that attracts birds. A good example of this shrub habitat is found around the Adams Street parking lot and in the broad swale below the trail leading to the bottom of the "H". Common birds in these areas are spotted and green-tailed towhees and chipping sparrows.

The spotted towhee, *Pipilo erythrophthalmus*, was formerly known as the rufous-sided towhee. The male's head and throat are black, appearing as if he is wearing a hood. His back and wings are also black, but spotted with white. The bird's breast is white and flanked with chestnut. The eye is red—hence the species name, which comes from the root words *erythros*, meaning "red," and *ophthalmos*, meaning "eye." The female towhee is a paler, browner version of the male. During breeding season, males are regularly seen displaying in the shrubs near the city's drinking water reservoir. Their song is a buzzy, rather unmusical chup chup zeeeeee.

The green-tailed towhee tends to prefer shrubby sites that are fairly dry. However, on Mount Helena both species can be found in the same habitat. Green-tails are reliably found in the shrubby swale below the "H".

The Birds of
MONTANA

BY S. S. HEALY

The Helena Independent,
Sunday July 23, 1905

There on the blasted top of that storm-smitten pine sit two Clarke's nutcrackers; one is this year's fledgeling and although as large as the mother bird, by whose side it is sitting, it shakes its wings and in pleading voice begs for bread. There in the top of that fragrant fir, near those great clusters of sweet-breathed syringas, a junco is chanting its "even-song." Assiduously and persistently some young chickadees are following the parent birds through the woods, calling for their evening meal. Up there on a higher pinnacle of rock a vesper sparrow sings to the setting sun; on swift and tireless wing the bi-color swallows are circling about the crags catching gnats and mosquitos and carrying them to their nestlings in the rocks.

The detonation of Fort Harrison's sunset gun reaches our ears and, taking another "pull" at our bottle—of water—we begin the descent.

On the way down a fine blue grouse (cock) is flushed, one of four adult birds located on the north slope of Mount Helena. These grouse are very tame and may be approached to within 15 yards. Gunner, please leave them alone. We will gladly buy you some meat rather than have those birds disturbed. It would be splendid to have a hundred grouse on Mount Helena; let us make it a game preserve.

Persons coming here from the east are wholly unacquainted with our large blue grouse. Do not interfere with game birds on Mount Helena and within three years we will have a splendid zoo amid its firs and crags. Go to the meat market and buy a soup bone.

Shame on the man who kills or drives those grouse away. ♦

The green-tailed towhee, *Pipilo chlorurus*, is smaller than the spotted towhee. The male is olive green on the back and tail. His head has a rusty cap, and his white chin and throat contrast with a gray breast. The green-tailed towhee's song begins with a clear whistle followed by a jumble of buzzy trills.

The chipping sparrow, *Spizella passerina*, is a small, gray-breasted sparrow with a light brown back. A fine, black stripe goes through the bird's eye, and a thin white eyebrow separates the black eyestripe from a bright chestnut-colored cap.

The chipping sparrow builds small, compact nests with linings of hair and fine grasses that are concealed in the interior of shrubs. When a person is in close proximity of a nest, these sparrows often respond by making a repeated short, sharp chip while excitedly moving from one perch to another. Perhaps this vocalization gave them their common name. The song of the chipping sparrow is a dry rattle, all on one pitch.

With a little extra effort, birders can also find calliope or rufous hummingbirds, dusky flycatchers, and lazuli buntings within the shrub habitat of Mount Helena.

BIRDS OF THE CONIFER FOREST

Beginning about midway up the north-facing slope of Mount Helena, Douglas-fir (in the cooler, wetter areas) and ponderosa pine (in drier areas) dominate the landscape. Most of these trees are young, having regrown since the mountain was largely denuded of trees during the early years of Helena. As a result, there are relatively few large trees or dead snags. Therefore, birds that prefer and depend on old-growth forest habitat are seen here infrequently. Birds such as downy and hairy woodpeckers, or even northern flickers, are uncommon.

The most commonly found, year-round residents are mountain chickadees, red-breasted nuthatches, golden-crowned kinglets, Townsend's solitaires, and juncos. During the nesting season the yellow-rumped warbler is also common over the entire forested area. Some species occur on specific areas of the mountain. To find the solitary vireo and Hammond's flycatcher, listen for them on the uphill side of the 1906 Trail leading to the "H". Hermit thrushes are found almost exclusively at or near the summit of the mountain on the north and west slopes.

Mountain chickadees, *Parus gambeli*, are similar in appearance, behavior, and vocalization to the black-capped chickadee, which is common in town and in the Helena Valley. They are small, only about 5 inches long. Light gray overall, the mountain chickadee has a black cap with a white eyebrow and a black stripe across the eye—something like a "Lone Ranger" mask. In contrast, the black-capped chickadee has a solid black cap extending below the eye.

Chickadees are name-sayers—in other words, their song says their name, chick-adee-adee-adee. With practice you

Nuthatches are cavity nesters.... They frequently smear pitch around the cavity opening, perhaps to discourage insects from entering.

can distinguish the nasal chick-adee-adee-adee of the mountain chickadee from the more clear song of the black-capped variety. Chickadees nest in cavities, such as nest boxes, abandoned nests of woodpeckers, or nests that they excavate themselves if they find a suitable tree with soft wood. Chickadees are permanent residents on Mount Helena. Except in the breeding season, when they pair off, both species are commonly observed traveling in small groups of six to twelve birds.

Red-breasted nuthatches, *Sitta canadensis*, are more frequently heard than they are seen. Nuthatches make a high, nasal enk, enk, enk, which may be heard throughout the year, but is heard more frequently during breeding season. The red-breasted nuthatch has a black cap and a gray back and tail. It has a white eyebrow and a black stripe through the eye. Its underparts from throat to tail are a rusty brown.

Nuthatches are easily identified by their distinctive feeding behavior. They feed from the bark of limbs and trunks of trees, usually moving down the trunk headfirst. They use their short, slim, pointed beak to probe the bark for insects. Nuthatches are also cavity nesters. They construct their own nest cavity and seldom reuse their old nests or nests of other birds. They frequently smear pitch around the cavity opening, perhaps to discourage insects from entering.

Townsend's solitaire, *Myadestes townsendi*, is a member of the thrush family and is another permanent resident of Mount Helena. This bird is

Townsend's solitaire
Myadestes townsendi
Illustration by
Peter Grosshauser

overall gray in color with buffy wing patches that are quite noticeable during flight. Its tail is long, with white outer tail feathers that are also noticeable during flight. While perched, a solitaire may display a series of quick "flashes" of these white tail feathers as a kind of territorial display. At close range, a fine, white eye ring can be seen on these birds.

Solitaires are ground nesters and select ledges or small cutbanks on which to place their nests. During warmer seasons, solitaires feed on insects, which they often capture by flycatching. They also stoop to insects after hovering in the air a few feet above the ground, diving to the ground to make a capture. In winter months these birds feed extensively on the cones or "berries" of junipers.

Solitaires maintain territories year-round although winter and breeding territories may not be the same. They give a short, mellow call that may be repeated for several minutes at a time. Solitaires call and sing throughout the year, typically from the top of tall trees. Their song is a loud, complex musical warble that may continue for several minutes. Any bird song heard during winter months on Mount Helena is almost certainly that of a solitaire.

The hermit thrush, *Catharus guttatus*, is a summer resident of the mountain. This thrush and other "spot-breasted" thrushes are known for their serene, flutelike songs. The hermit thrush is secretive and, even though

37

it may be common, is often difficult to observe. The back of the hermit thrush is a medium gray, and the rump and tail are a rusty brown. The bird's breast is light gray and spotted with distinct medium brown spots. When at rest, the hermit's wingtips appear to droop below its tail. The behavior of cocking its tail and slowly dropping it is characteristic.

Two other spot-breasted thrushes very similar in appearance are found in the Helena area—the Swainson's thrush and the veery. Their songs are similar, but different in pattern. The hermit thrush's song first ascends, then descends in pitch. The Swainson's thrush makes an ascending song, and the veery sings a descending song. Both Swainson's and hermit thrushes may be closely associated in similar habitat. The veery is found only in deciduous riparian habitat along streams and rivers.

BIRDS OF CLIFFS AND ROCK OUTCROPS

The limestone cliffs and rock outcrops at Mount Helena's summit provide essential habitat for rock wrens, *Salpinctes obsoletus*. Although these birds are more abundant near the rock outcrops at the bottom of Grizzly Gulch just southeast of the park, a few wrens are regular nesters around the mountain's summit.

Wrens in general are vociferous songsters. Their songs are usually loud and bubbly, filled with buzzes and trills. The rock wren is no exception, calling out an energetic series of chew, chew, chew . . . chub, chub, chub . . . zwee, zwee, zwee . . . all at different pitches. Characteristic of most wrens, the rock wrens hold their bodies parallel to the ground and often cock their tails vertically. Rock wrens are pale gray below and gray to brown above. Their bill is slender and pointed. Nests are placed in a rock crevice or under rock ledges, and the nest entrance is often paved with small pebbles. They are aggressive and very territorial.

Wrens in general are vociferous songsters. Their songs are usually loud and bubbly, filled with buzzes and trills.

A family of ravens are fairly regular nesters in cavities or on protected ledges in the mountain's large north-facing cliffs. The common raven, *Corvus corax,* is the largest member of the crow family. It is totally black in color, has a heavy, thick bill, and throat feathers of a shaggy appearance. This largest member of the songbird family has a croaky and metallic rather than musical voice, but does have an expansive and expressive

Birding Mount Helena is a pleasure, not so much for the birds seen, but for the aesthetics of the outing.

vocabulary of sounds. Ravens can be distinguished from smaller, sleeker American crows by the crows' clear calls of caw, caw, caw.

Ravens are predominately scavengers but also prey on small mammals and birds and bird nests. Before the 1950s ravens were seldom seen near human development and were considered a wilderness species. As inroads have been made in wild areas, ravens have adapted to human activities and settlements. Now they are common throughout the intermontane valleys and find food from a variety of human sources, including road-killed animals and landfills.

In the past, prairie falcons have also nested on the cliffs of Mount Helena. Probably because of disturbance and habitat changes in the Helena Valley, there have been no recent nesting attempts. However, transient falcons may be seen occasionally at any time of the year.

Falcons as a group are streamlined, swift fliers with long pointed wings and a longish tail. The prairie falcon is brown overall with a streaked breast. The most reliable identifying marks of this falcon are the black patches in the wingpits, seen during flight. The falcon's voice is a high pitched, rapid series of kee, kee, kee, kees that is often heard in the vicinity of a nest site. Prairie falcons are primarily predators of other birds, which they pursue and capture in the air.

At the north and east boundaries of Mount Helena, where the mountain slopes abut the city environment, a few "town" birds spill into the park. These birds include barn and tree swallows, starlings, house finches, and house sparrows.

SEASONAL SIGHTINGS

The numbers and species of birds found on Mount Helena vary with the season. The greatest number of bird species will be found there from May to July, when summer residents have returned from their winter habitats in the southern United States, Mexico, Central America, and even farther south. Spring arrival of these migratory birds doubles the number of species found on the mountain during the winter months.

Spring displays, such as singing and colorful breeding plumage displayed by the males of many species, occur only during the breeding season and make birds more noticeable. By July, many birds have become quiet and secretive. Males are no longer attracting females, and individuals or families survive by being less obvious to predators. During mid- to late summer, birds of all ages are concerned with growth and accumulating energy reserves.

In August, the summer residents begin returning to their winter habitats. By the end of September, only the resident birds remain. These year-round species tend to be quiet and inconspicuous. Compiling a respectable bird list at this time takes more patience and effort. But winter birding on Mount Helena may result in bird observations that are unlikely at other times of the year—you may see gray and Steller's jays, or rosy finches.

A close and easy complement to birding Mount Helena is a drive up Grizzly Gulch. This area is reached by following Park Avenue south past Reeder's Alley to the edge of town. Take the right or west fork at the "Y." A sign is also here. Grizzly Gulch has cottonwood and aspen along its bottom and conifers along its sides that tend to be older and larger than those found on Mount Helena. Stops along the road can add several species to your list, including ruffed grouse, red-naped sapsucker, house wren, Swainson's thrush, warbling vireo, orange-crowned warbler, and yellow warbler.

A short walk into Mount Helena Park leaves the bustle of the city and much of the noise behind. Birding Mount Helena is a pleasure, not so much for the birds seen, but for the aesthetics of the outing. You will find, particularly if you go during the morning hours, that you are often alone. The city noises are distant, and, even if the birds are not cooperative, you will be transfixed by the views.

BUGS AND BUTTERFLIES

by Bea Vogel

ount Helena abounds with insects—grasshoppers, bees, ants, butterflies, moths, beetles, ground beetles, tiger beetles, crickets, true flies, lacewing flies, wasps, true bugs, leaf hoppers, aphids, earwigs, spring tails, and more. There are probably at least thirty insect species for each vertebrate species (mammals, birds, reptiles, and amphibians). For this and other reasons listed below, it is not possible to list all the insect species of Mount Helena:

1) Except for butterflies, there are no field guides or handbooks for insect species; existing guides name only families, two ranks above species.

2) What we think of as insects are just the adult stage of an organism, usually short-lived. Adults live perhaps a day, or at most 2 or 3 weeks. The rest of the year is spent in a dormant stage as an egg or pupa, or in the feeding stage, which for many insects is a wormlike grub.

3) The great majority of insects that live on Mount Helena are small, less than 0.5 inch long, and are likely to be overlooked. They may hide under grass and dried vegetation, on the undersides of leaves and on plant stems, under stones and logs, or even underground. Many insects that feed on plants cannot remain hidden, but they remain unnoticed by resembling the leaves they eat, or by moving so slowly that our impatient vertebrate eyes pass over them.

4) In general the insects of the Rocky Mountains are poorly studied, and many have no name because they have not been scientifically described. Butterflies, alone among the many orders of insects, are the exception.

Since a comprehensive look at all of Mount Helena's insect communities is beyond the scope of this guide, this chapter will talk about the mountain's most visible and beautiful insects—butterflies.

MOUNT HELENA BUTTERFLIES

Among the hundreds of insects that live on Mount Helena, butterflies are probably the only ones that delight most people. Their colorful flight pleases the eye, and they do not appear to be pests. Many butterflies are brightly patterned and others can be seen on warm, sunny days from early spring until late fall.

Butterflies are the adult form of an insect that spends much of its life as a caterpillar. As adults, they spend their time flying around to find a mate, to find a plant on which to lay eggs, or to visit a flower for nectar to drink for energy. An excellent place to look for butterflies is a patch of flowers with nectaries, such as clover, thistle, and even knapweed.

The largest butterfly found on Mount Helena is the Two-Tailed Tiger Swallowtail, which patrols trails. It is bright yellow with black stripes, and can be as large as the palm of a human hand. Good places to look for this butterfly are the 1906 Trail and the Charcoal Kiln ravine. Swallowtails are also seen all over the town of Helena because their food plants include chokecherry, ash, and poplar.

Two-Tailed Tiger Swallowtail
Illustration by Bea Vogel.

Another largeish butterfly, though smaller than a swallowtail, seen in the Charcoal Kiln ravine is the White Admiral. The White Admiral's upperside is black with a broad white band. Its underside also shows the white band, but the rest of its underwing is patterned black and orange. Admirals spend less time flying than they do sitting on bushes about 8 feet above the ground.

Three of the butterfly species found on Mount Helena overwinter as adults and may be seen as early as February on warm, sunny days. The Mourning Cloak is a dark brown or black with a white or creamy border on the upperside of the wing. If you happen to see one of these butterflies perched, instead of flying, you might notice a band of blue dots next to the light band. Tortoiseshells and Anglewings also may be seen early in the year. The underside of both is dull brown. If one of these butterflies is seated with its wings folded up over its back, it looks like a dried leaf.

The upperside of the Anglewing is bright orange or even red with brown and yellow markings. The upperside of the Tortoiseshell wing is much darker, but has a strong band of orange and yellow at its edge. The wing margin of both is a toothed, not a smooth, curve. All three of these early spring fliers may be seen throughout the season.

A few other butterflies are also brightly colored and catch the eye. Sulphurs, as the name suggests, are bright yellow, about half the size of swallowtails, and are often seen feeding on yellow flowers. Sulphurs have no conspicuous patterns unless seen close up.

Two or three species of white butterflies, which are cousins of Sulphurs, have also been seen on Mount Helena. The Cabbage White is nearly all white; Checkered or Western Whites have blackish or greenish checkerboard patterns on their wings. If you are lucky, you may see one of the loveliest butterflies in the park, an Orangetip, flying rapidly through a sunny forest patch. It is a smallish white butterfly with a bright orange triangular patch at the tip of its forewing.

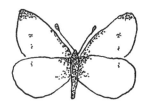

Western White
Illustration by Bea Vogel.

Other "Oh my!" butterflies are small blue butterflies that flash breathtaking iridescent color. They are referred to collectively as "blues." There are three or four species of these butterflies in the park, but they are not easy to distinguish without close examination. Generally, male blues are more brightly colored; some female blues are even brown.

There are several orange or reddish patterned butterflies. Fritillaries have an orange and black checkerboard pattern on the upper side of their wings. Greater Fritillaries have silver spots on the underside, but on Lesser Fritillaries both sides of the wing are similar.

Painted Ladies, which occasionally are seen in great abundance, are reddish orange on the upperside with a black patch at the wingtip, marked with white spots. Their underside is a brown and white "map" pattern, with some pink on the underside of the forewing.

Several dull or dark-colored butterflies skulk in tall grass and in the shade of shrubs. The largest of these is the Large Wood Nymph, which is dark brown with conspicuous eyespots on the underside of its forewing. Entomologists think that these eyespots make a butterfly look like a rodent—something too large for a butterfly-eating bird to feed on.

ANTS
— of —
MOUNT
HELENA

BY BEA VOGEL

Mounds of finely cut vegetation can be seen on the lower slopes of Mount Helena and in the park's open ponderosa pine forests. Each is a city of mound-building ants. Each mound, which may be more than a foot high, is constructed of pine needles, grass stems, and twigs patterned into a thatch.

Ants have attracted much attention because of their social nature, many working together for their common survival. On the mounds, the visible ants are workers—nonreproductive adults, children of a single reproductive adult, or slaves captured by raids on other ant colonies.

Not all ants on Mount Helena build mounds. Some "anthills" are indicated only by a patch of fine gravel around their entrances. Almost all anthills have some sort of built structure. The mound seems to serve some sophisticated method of controlling temperature within the colony. The sloped sides can absorb much more of the sun's heat than a flat surface can, and the thatch is better insulation than gravel or earth. Inside the mound are carefully constructed chambers and passages. The workers attend the young of the colony and the eggs, larvae, and pupae, moving them up into the mound chambers when the sun warms them or down into the lower levels to escape extremes of heat or cold.

Workers also gather food for the colony, including seeds and perhaps insects. Some of the food is used for maintaining workers, some is stored for other seasons. Much of it is chewed up to make pabulum for the larvae.

To damage or disturb an ant mound is like Godzilla attacking Helena, smashing buildings and residents alike. It is thoughtlessly cruel and unnecessary. Observe these busy creatures without disturbing their homes. ◆

The Common Alpine is a dark brown to black-looking butterfly that is quite abundant on the mountain's lower slopes, darting in and around bushes. Two species of ringlet also dance and flutter on the grassy lower slopes. Ringlets derive their name from a small black eyespot near the tip of their forewing, although not all butterflies in this group are so marked. The Ochre Ringlet is a light grayish tan on its underside, and more orangish on the upperside, without any distinct pattern other than the ringlet spot. Hayden's Ringlet is a dull tan or gray with no markings on the upperside, but the underside of its hindwing has a row of black eyespots—each with a light center and surrounded by a golden ring. Although all the other butterflies mentioned here are quite common and widely distributed in the West, Hayden's Ringlet is found only along the eastern slope of the Rocky Mountains from the Tetons north to Lincoln, Montana, but is not rare within its range.

Mount Helena is also home to several species of skippers. Although they are mothlike in appearance and flight, they are active in the daytime like other butterflies. These insects are smallish and often sit on bare ground. One group of skippers is a mottled orangish color, with a characteristic way of holding its wings. A butterfly keeps its forewing and hindwing in the same plane, either spread flat or folded vertically over its back. The orange skippers sit with forewing and hindwing in different planes, so it is obvious they have four wings. When they fly they seem to hop or skip jerkily, rather than slide. Another group of skippers are dark brown or gray, sometimes with tiny white dots. These skippers also sit on bare ground, but hold their wings spread flat.

Milbert's Tortoiseshell
Illustration by Bea Vogel.

Altogether there are probably twenty to twenty-five species of butterflies, including skippers, found on Mount Helena.

FACTS
— about —
TICKS

BY BEA VOGEL

Ticks are active in spring and early summer and may annoy Mount Helena hikers by attaching themselves to human bodies. Ticks are not insects, but are semi-parasitic arachnids with eight legs and a single body part. They are small, lentil-shaped animals, and the female of the species is obliged to have a meal of mammal blood to reproduce. Although a few ticks carry nasty diseases such as Rocky Mountain spotted fever or Lyme disease, most ticks do more insult than injury.

Ticks wait on shrubs and bushes near trails, hoping a mammal will brush by. They seem to be attracted by body heat and motion. Once a tick attaches itself to a person it wanders around, often for hours, looking for the optimum place to attach—moist, hairy places like the groin, under a waistband, or the hairline on the back of the neck. The tick saws through the skin with its serrated mouthparts. These serrations are designed to firmly anchor the tick so it cannot be brushed off.

If you find a tick imbedded in your skin, remove it carefully and without panic so that no mouthparts are left behind to cause an infection. The best method of removal is to grasp the tick gently and lift its body until there is a slight pull on the skin. Then wait. The tick will work itself free. It can then be disposed of by drowning it in rubbing alcohol or flushing it down the toilet. Do not apply alcohol to a tick until it is free from your body. Do not apply heat or stab it with a pin. If you kill the tick before it has released itself, parts of it will remain in your skin.

After a spring walk on Mount Helena, a tick inspection is a good idea. Remove all your clothing and, with the help of mirrors or another person, inspect your body carefully. The tick(s) may not have attached—these are easy to remove. Then wash all your clothes immediately. Detergent and washing will probably kill ticks, but if you wear the same clothes again without washing—even days later— the ticks may still be there, waiting patiently for you to do so. ♦

PLANTS AND PLANT COMMUNITIES

◆

H. Wayne Phillips

From the majesty of towering forest trees to the beauty and wonder of the tiniest wildflower, the diverse native plant life of Mount Helena City Park is a major attraction for visitors. There are more than 220 plant species growing on Mount Helena.

The vascular plant list in the Appendix includes 3 forest tree species, 31 woody shrubs, 28 grass and grasslike plants, and 158 wildflowers and herbs that are known to occur on the mountain. Also occurring are numerous mosses and lichens.

These plants occur on a landscape that varies in response to habitat conditions such as elevation, soil, exposure to the sun, and the dynamics of fire, wind, flood, and drought. For example, some plants require the warm, direct sunlight of a southern exposure, while others prefer the cool, indirect rays of sunlight that filter through the tree canopy to the forest floor. The varied landscape of Mount Helena, from rock cliff to mountain slope, provides habitat for a varied and interesting flora, distributed on the mountain in recognizable plant communities. The major plant communities on Mount Helena include: ponderosa pine woodlands, Douglas-fir forests, grasslands and shrublands, tall shrub draws, and cliff/rock outcrop vegetation.

Despite the seemingly serene beauty of Mount Helena's plant life, there are concerns about its future. Noxious weeds are spreading and, if not controlled, could reduce native wildflowers and eventually dominate the landscape. Trees, once thought to be too few, are now becoming overly

abundant. Dense young trees have spread into areas that were open grasslands only a decade or two ago, reducing plant diversity and increasing fire hazard. Fire, always considered a threat, is increasingly so, as new tree growth extends down to city streets. Fortunately, the City of Helena has a management plan for the park to deal with these problems, and the park has many friends among the city's citizens. Working together with nature, the beauty of Mount Helena's diverse plant life will persist for generations to come.

Ponderosa pine. Wayne Philips photo.

PONDEROSA PINE WOODLAND

Ponderosa pine trees are the dominant feature of the most abundant and easily recognized plant community on the mountain. Ponderosa pine is the state tree of Montana, and it is widespread in the lower elevation forests of the state. Pine trees have their needles arranged in neat little bundles, as if held together by a band of gray thread at the base of the needles. The long needles of ponderosa pine normally occur in bundles of three. In contrast, the shorter needles of limber pine occur in bundles of five. Limber pine often occurs with ponderosa pine on rocky and wind-exposed places on the mountain.

Ponderosa pine communities are most common on the south half of the park traversed by the Prospect Shafts Trail and the Back Side Trail. The spacing of trees varies from rather dense forest/shrub communities on the cooler northeastern exposures, to woodlands of more widely spaced pine trees on the dry, grassy slopes of southern and western exposures of the mountain. On cool spring and fall days, I like to hike on these "high energy" slopes of

48

the mountain, to maximize my exposure to the warm rays of the sun.

Bitterbrush and bluebunch wheatgrass often occur together with ponderosa pine in these communities. Look for the bright yellow, sunflower-like blossoms and large arrowhead-shaped leaves of arrowleaf balsamroot beneath open-growing pine trees in early summer.

DOUGLAS-FIR FORESTS

The steeper and more sheltered north and east-facing slopes of the mountain are clothed in a dark green canopy of Douglas-fir trees. Most of these trees started their growth during the earliest years of the city of Helena. Among them are trees which were planted in 1906 by Helena National Forest employees under the direction of Forest Assistant Bond, at the request of the members of the Helena Improvement Society.

The easiest way to experience the Douglas-fir forest is to hike the 1906 Trail. After passing underneath the "H" we enter the dense Douglas-fir forest. The aroma of fir needles and the cool air here reminds us of the change in the environment beneath the forest canopy. On hot summer days, young adventure seekers often head for "Devil's Kitchen Cave" and linger in the refreshing coolness of the shade under the dense forest beneath the cliffs.

With the limited light filtering through the trees, the forest floor vegetation here is sparse. Thriving are shade-tolerant low shrubs like shiny-leaf spirea, russet buffalo-berry, and snowberry. The tiny white flowers of false Solomon's seal and fairy bells, found here in spring, turn to a cluster of reddish berries by late summer. The purple flowers of showy aster can be found in late summer or early fall.

GRASSLANDS AND SHRUBLANDS

The lower northeastern slopes of Mount Helena, from the Adams Street Trailhead to the North Access Trail, are dominated by mountain bunchgrass vegetation, often in combination with low, woody shrubs. On cool north- and east-facing slopes, rough fescue and Idaho fescue are the major grasses. On south-facing slopes, bluebunch wheatgrass, Montana's state grass, is more common. The showy, open seed arrangements of Indian ricegrass can be found on the driest and warmest exposures.

PLANT COMMUNITIES *of* MOUNT HELENA

- Douglas-fir forest
- Ponderosa pine woodland
- Grasslands and shrublands
- Grassland/forest in transition
- Cliffs and rock outcrops
- Tall shrub draw

REBER PARK ADDITION

Panhandle Trail

North Access Trail

Quaking Trail

Sunset Point

Prairie Trail

0.8

0.4

Devil's Kitchen

1906 Trail 0.9

Radio Tower
5,320'
North Summit

Limestone Cliffs

0.1

0.4

MT. HELENA
5,460'
South Summit

5360'
5280'
5200'
5120'
5040'
4960' 4880'

Hogback Trail 0.3

West End Trail

0.4

Backside Trail 0.5

Prospect Shafts

Mt. Helena Ridge National Recreation Trail

5.0 miles from park boundary to Park City Trailhead

HELENA NATIONAL FOREST

GLENDALE
GARRISON
MTN VIEW
CHARLIE RUSSELL DRIVE
MT. HELENA DRIVE

N

0   0.25   0.5

Miles

50

One of the last wildflowers to bloom ... is dotted blazingstar. Its upright spike of bright magenta flowers sharply contrasts with the dry, straw-colored grasses in late August and September.

Bitterbrush, with its tiny, fragrant, yellow blossoms, is the most abundant low growing woody plant of the shrublands. Along the Prairie Trail, large areas of bitterbrush can be seen. Deer relish browsing on the nutritious twigs and leaves of this shrub, especially in the winter. You can recognize bitterbrush by the small, three-lobed, non-aromatic leaves. Sagebrush also has three-lobed leaves, but with a distinctive pungent aroma of "sage." Another common shrub, skunkbush sumac, has three separate leaflets, joined at the base, and a cluster of bright red, berry-like fruit.

Wildflowers in the grasslands and shrublands are abundant. Blue flax, larkspur, harebell, chickweed, scarlet gaura, wavy-leaved thistle, prairie smoke, and many more, bloom from early spring to fall. In early spring, the Montana state wildflower, the bitterroot, can be found in a small grassy park at the junction of the Back Side Trail and the Prairie Trail. One of the last wildflowers to bloom in the grasslands is dotted blazingstar. Its upright spike of bright magenta flowers sharply contrasts with the dry, straw-colored grasses in late August and September.

GRASSLAND/FOREST IN TRANSITION

The "Prairie" Trail from the Adams Street Trailhead west to Sunset Point may need a name change in future decades. This trail skirts the edge of the Douglas-fir forest passing through newly developing young tree growth interspersed with bunchgrass and low shrubs. These young, Christmas tree-size Douglas-fir and ponderosa pine trees have established themselves in the open grassy slopes in recent years. From the seed dispersed by wind and gravity from the mature trees nearby, a new forest is emerging. The abundant small trees became established when good cone-producing years on the mountain were followed by moist growing seasons, allowing new trees to get started in the "prairie."

The process of one plant community (forest) replacing another (grassland/shrubland) is called plant succession. Unless the process is reversed by fire, insect epidemic, or thinning, plant succession will continue to progress on the mountain, from grassland to forest. Trees and associated shade-tolerant vegetation will gradually replace the sun-loving plants of the open, grassy slopes. In time, these north slopes may become a dense, shady forest much like the Douglas-fir forest that can be seen on the slopes above. Then, "Forest" Trail may be a more appropriate name for the trail.

For now, the area is a forest in transition. The young fir and pine tress share the slope with a diverse mixture of fescue grasses, bitterbrush, rabbitbrush, and many wildflowers. The colorful blossoms of lupine, blanket flower, pussytoes, harebell, sugarbowl, prairiesmoke, and mountain bluebells bloom in profusion in early summer.

TALL SHRUB DRAWS

The vegetation in the steep draw bottoms is often similar to riparian vegetation found along streams, although there is no surface water on the mountain, except during rainstorms. The tall deciduous shrubs that grow in the draws have their roots deep in the sub-surface moisture. Mountain maple, serviceberry, and chokecherry, the tallest shrubs of the draws, may reach a height of more than ten feet. Intermediate size shrubs from three to six feet tall include mock orange, skunkbush sumac, and currant. Low-growing snowberry and the showy, purple blossoms of clematis vines thrive in the shelter of the tall shrubs. Look closely to be rewarded with small, but sweet, wild strawberries.

A tall shrub draw is the first feature crossed as you leave the Adams Street trailhead, heading up the 1906 Trail, on your left opposite the water tanks. You can also find the tall shrub draw communities near the lime kilns along the Prospect Shafts Trail on the southeast side of the park, and along the 1906 Trail near the "H." These communities are especially important to songbirds, and many species nest here. It is a good place to see and hear birds, but be careful not to disturb them.

CLIFF AND ROCK OUTCROP VEGETATION

On the rocky summits, ridgetops, and limestone cliffs, the elements are at their fiercest. Soil and moisture to support plant growth is scarce. Wind is constant, rapidly sucking away what little moisture does collect. Only plants

Wild
PLANT OBSERVATION

BY BONNIE HEIDEL

LIME KILNS—Many points along Mount Helena's trails are excellent viewing sites for plants. Many wild plants need wet conditions that saturate the ground or keep it damp during parts of the growing season. Drainage bottoms like this are luxuriant slivers of habitat for plants found nowhere else on the mountain.

PROSPECT SHAFTS RIDGE—Mount Helena is thin-skinned on ridgelines, summits, and other exposed places where its shallow mantle of soil is interrupted by bedrock at the surface. The extensive calcareous bedrock makes many of these places prime real estate for plants that favor calcareous conditions.

LOWER NORTH ACCESS—Large areas of Mount Helena's north-facing slopes are dotted by young Douglas-firs and ponderosa pines.

BITTERROOT MEADOWS—Meet three Montana mascots in one place. Bitterroot is the state wildflower, Ponderosa pine is the state tree, and bluebunch wheatgrass is the state grass. It is up to today's Montanans to leave bitterroot growing in the wild for future generations. Please do not pick these flowers. The Montana mascots share this ridge where lightning has left its signature on trees.

DEVIL'S KITCHEN—Devil's Kitchen is carved out of Mount Helena's largest cliff, an abrupt wall of rock. The cliff has created a fire shadow where trees have historically been sheltered from the mountain's periodic fires. Most trees in this area larger than 6 inches in diameter began growing before turn-of-the-century wildfires burned most of the Mount Helena timber.

THE HELENA VALLEY—The sweep of the Helena Valley stretching before you represents what was once a dry, intermontane grassland laced with waterways. It was a favorite haunt of bison herds.

SOUTH END TRAIL JUNCTION—A war is being played out here. Dalmatian toadflax is a striking, yellow-flowered perennial that grows wild in the Balkans. It was brought to Helena and other American places for use in gardens, as decoration. From there it escaped into the wild, where it has become an aggressive weed that outcompetes wild plants, diminishing land and forage values. It is the single most widespread weed on Mount Helena.

DO NOT PICK THESE YELLOW FLOWERS! Various organisms that keep it in check in the Balkans are being enlisted for trial in Helena.

PRAIRIE TRAIL KNOLL—Colorful cushion plant communities lure hikers to this north-mountain knoll. Deep roots, ground-hugging mats, and early flowering enable these plants to survive the wind's scourge. Among these low-growing flowers are a beguiling forget-me-not, tufted milkvetch, and a yellow, daisy-like flower, cushion goldenweed.

BACK SIDE TRAIL JUNCTION—Glance downslope and you will see fire scars on the tree trunks facing you, indicating an uphill ground fire. Look across the ravine for the color and texture differences of ponderosa pine and Douglas-fir, with the more drought-tolerant pine at both the top and bottom of the slope.

WEST SIDE SADDLE—For elk, the bitterbrush on these calcareous slopes and winterfat in the shale outcrops provide winter forage. A great many of Mount Helena's wild plants have food or medicinal values for humans, too.

THE HELENA BENCH—Helena is nestled along the margin between mountains and valley, on an elongate bench. Life on the sheltered edge between mountain and valley has an overlapping bounty. Helena's "earliest residents" included wild plants and animals from both settings.

THE SOUTH HILLS—Grassy knolls and a mantle of dry conifer forest mark the upper limits of Helena.

THE SCRATCHGRAVEL HILLS—The dark islands of jutting hills that lie north of Mount Helena are the Scratchgravel Hills, covered by dry pine forest. They mirror the dry forests south of Helena that grow on sterile soils formed from the Boulder Batholith.

BIG BELT MOUNTAINS—The Helena Valley melts into mountain vistas where foothills meet forests of ponderosa pine, lodgepole pine, and Douglas-fir. These are the most common forests east of the Continental Divide. Forest gives way to high meadow ridges and rocky alpine summits of the Big Belt Mountains across the eastern horizonline.

THE VIEW FROM THE SUMMIT—The summit panorama is adorned with plant life repeating and expanding on the patterns found on Mount Helena. More than 600 species of vascular plants grow wild throughout the valley and surrounding mountains. ♦

Douglas-fir.
Wayne Phillips photo.

with special adaptations to harsh conditions thrive here. The dense mats of tiny cushion plants survive by hugging the surface between the rocks, only inches high. The compactness of these cushions affords them protection from the wind and conserves moisture. Their short flowering and fruiting season allows them to complete their annual cycle while moisture is available in the spring, and then to go dormant during the summer drought.

You can find these specialized little cushion plants on the rocky ridge of the Prospect Shafts Trail, the Hogback Trail to the Mount Helena summit, midway on the Prairie Trail and on the top of the limestone cliffs that form the Mount Helena face. Often, isolated limber pine trees also grow in the rocky soil in stunted gnarly forms, much like the "bonsai" trees of Japanese gardens. Among the plants that grow as cushions are tufted milk-vetch, Douglasia, Hooker's townsendia, Howard's forget-me-not, alpine bladderpod, cut-leaved fleabane, cushion buckwheat, stemless hymenoxys, paronychia, Hood's phlox, and lance-leaved stonecrop.

Perhaps the showiest of the cushion plants is Douglasia. The small, deep purple flowers of Douglasia so densely cover the phlox-like cushions of this plant that the small leaves can scarcely be seen. After the drabness of winter, these vividly colored flowers are a welcome confirmation that spring has arrived at last.

Hooker's townsendia, also known as Easter daisy, with its large, white heads, blooms about the same time as Douglasia, in April, near the Easter holiday. The clusters of white Easter daisy flowers thrust upward out of cracks in the limestone rocks, sometimes masked by the snow that pelts down in the spring squalls. But when the fickle sun melts the snow, the bright, white flowers can surprise the hiker with their size and beauty.

Besides the cushion plants, other woody species adapt to the rocks by plunging their taproots deep into rocky crevices. Limber pine and wax currant, for example, grow out of cliff faces and other rocky exposures. The sheer, north-facing cliffs below the summit of Mount Helena have their own calcium-loving plants that are shade tolerant, like lip-fern.

After the drabness of winter, these vividly colored flowers are a welcome confirmation that spring has arrived at last.

Although the plants of the cliffs and rock outcrops appear hardy, they are very slow-growing and difficult to reestablish once lost. For example, the rocky summit of Mount Helena is becoming depleted of cushion plant vegetation because of heavy traffic there. Please stay on the trails to avoid crushing these tiny plants with your boots.

NATIVE PLANTS, EXOTIC PLANTS, AND NOXIOUS WEEDS

The plant list in the Appendix distinguishes between plants that are native and those that are exotic. Native plants are those which we believe were growing here when Lewis and Clark came up the Missouri River in 1805. In contrast, exotic species have been introduced here from another continent, like Siberian wheatgrass, or even another area on this continent, like Kentucky bluegrass. Some exotic species are considered "noxious weeds," a term defined by law as a plant which may render land "unfit for agriculture or other beneficial uses." Noxious weeds occurring on Mount Helena include spotted knapweed, diffuse knapweed, leafy spurge, dalmatian toadflax, and Canada thistle. These noxious weeds aggresively compete with native plants for growing space and could become the dominant feature of the herbaceous vegetation, if not controlled.

If you would like to help promote the native wildflowers on the mountain by helping to control noxious weeds, you can:

1) Learn to distinguish the noxious weeds from the native wildflowers.

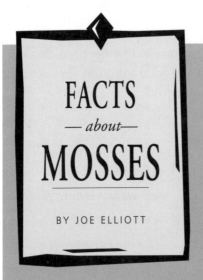

FACTS
— about —
MOSSES

BY JOE ELLIOTT

Mosses of Mount Helena grow mostly on the calcium-rich rocks and soils on north-facing slopes. The forest floor along shaded portions of the 1906 Trail has evergreen feather mosses that grow in clumps that are easily torn when walked on. The most common moss is *Abietinella abietina,* with lesser amounts of *Homalothecium nevadense,* a golden yellow moss with curled stems growing only on rock; *Brachythecium albicans; Pylaisiella polyantha;* and *Brachythecium collinum.*

Other common mosses have single, upright stems and often form cushions on soil, rock, and humus. These mosses include the following soil-growing species: *Timmia austriaca, Tortula ruralis, Tortula mucronifolia, Polytrichum juniperum, Pohia nutans, Bryum caespiticun,* and *Encalypta vulgaris.* Small blackish clumps of moss, forming round, velvety colonies on rock, belong to the genus *Grimmia,* which along with lichens are the first life to grow on rock outcrops. ◆

A flyer describing Mount Helena's noxious weeds is available and the Lewis and Clark County Agricultural Agent has information to help you identify them. Several good wildflower books are available to assist in learning to identify the wildflowers (see Selected References).

2) Please don't pick flowers in Mount Helena Park. Spotted knapweed and dalmatian toadflax have pretty, colorful flowers, and their dry seedheads make attractive dried-flower arrangements. However, picking the flowers or dry pods of these noxious weeds can spread their seed about the mountain and elsewhere. Picking the flowers and seedheads of native wildflowers prevents other visitors from enjoying their beauty and reduces the seed available for reproduction. Please do not pick flowers or seedheads of any plants on the mountain, except as explained in "3" below.

Spotted knapweed   *Dalmatian toadflax*

3) When you go on a hike, take along a plastic garbage bag, pull out the noxious weeds (roots and all), seal the bag so that seed cannot escape, and dispose of them in a dumpster. Time your weed-control trip following a rainstorm, when the soil is moist, for easier weed pulling. Taprooted species, like spotted knapweed, are much easier to pull than weeds with underground runners, like dalmatian toadflax. However, removal of the above or below ground portions of any noxious weed in this manner will help reduce the further spread of these undesirable plants.

4) Noxious weeds like disturbed, bare soil. By limiting your foot and mountain bike travel to the existing, marked trails, you will avoid disturbing the soil and making a home for more noxious weeds.

RARE PLANTS

Most of the native plant species on Mount Helena are representative of the dry forest, mountain bunchgrass, and shrubland vegetation that is found in similar settings elsewhere in Montana and in adjacent states. However, there are a few unique and rare species of native plants growing in the city park. For example, lesser rushy milkvetch, *Astragalus convallarius,* found in the park and in the Helena Valley, is known to be from only one other area in Montana. It is a Great Basin species at its northernmost limits. The rabbit's-foot crazyweed, *Oxytropis lagopus* var. *conjugens*, on Mount Helena, is rarer still, growing just in Montana and in a corner of Alberta. By staying on the trails and not picking wildflowers, you will be doing your part to protect the rare plants, as well as the more common plants, for all to enjoy.

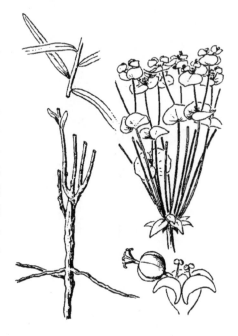

Leafy spurge

VEGETATION HISTORY AND THE ROLE OF FIRE

The forests and grasslands of Mount Helena are dynamic, in an ever-changing state of flux, unlike the rock face of the mountain. Many natural forces interact to bring about the dynamic vegetation changes; perhaps the most dramatic of these forces is wildfire. By studying fire scars and tree rings, forest scientists have determined that wildfire played a major role in the vegetation development of the forests in Montana, including Mount Helena, long before gold was discovered at Last Chance Gulch. Lightning, and perhaps Native Americans as well, started fires that swept these low elevation, dry forests at intervals of from five to twenty years.

When fires burned this frequently, they were low in intensity, normally burning mainly the vegetation and dried plant material at ground-line. Small trees were consumed or thinned, leaving large openings clear of trees entirely. Larger, more fire resistant trees survived the fires as widely spaced individuals and groups of trees. Many of the larger trees in the park today bear testimony to historic fires by their fire scars, most often on the uphill side of the tree. These open-canopy forests, interspersed with grassy parks, had relatively low fire hazards. The short intervals between fires prevented the development of thick, closed-canopy forests with heavy woody fuels—high fire hazards that are seen on the mountain today.

Old photographs show us that Mount Helena, in the early days of the city, had large, widely spaced trees, in a savannah or parkland structure, rather than in a dense forest. Many of those trees were logged until few were left. This depletion concerned many of the people of Helena, and they organized to reforest the mountain and create a city park.

Since those early days of park development, efforts have been made to quickly suppress all fires on Mount Helena, despite the lightning bolts that continue to pound the mountain and the visitors who are sometimes careless with matches.

As firefighters have become more successful in putting out fires, the vegetation balance has shifted in favor of the trees. Young trees have spread into areas formerly occupied by grassland and shrubland plant communities. For example, in the last twenty years the north slope of Mount Helena, above Le Grande Cannon Boulevard, has changed from a grassy slope, with a few isolated patches of trees, to an almost continuous forest of young tree seedlings and saplings (see photos in Introduction, pages 6 and 8). In the absence of natural fire cycles, insect epidemics, or human intervention, the trees will continue to spread, eventually developing a thick, closed-canopy forest, like the one you can see now under the cliffs.

When this happens, the tree canopies will block the reach of the sun to the forest floor. The prairie wildflowers that prefer full sunlight will decline. As flammable, woody material accumulates and the forest becomes more dense, the park will become more vulnerable to a large, severe fire that is more difficult for firefighters to control. A severe wildfire, burning under dry conditions, could sweep the mountain clear of trees, returning the mountain to a treeless state, as it was at the turn of the twentieth century.

The Mount Helena Park Management Plan, adopted by the City of Helena in November 1995, recognizes the increasing fire hazard on the mountain with advancing forest succession. The Plan states: "Over the long-term, vegetation will need to be actively managed to reduce fire hazards. Fire suppression will include thinning of tree stands." So the Park

Since those early days ... efforts have been made to quickly suppress all fires on Mt. Helena, despite the lightning bolts that continue to pound the mountain, and the visitors who are sometimes careless with matches.

61

Burned area on Mount Helena. Wayne Philips photo.

Management Plan calls for reducing the hazard of catastrophic wildfire by thinning the trees—ironic after the early day efforts to reforest the mountain. Thinning the trees would not only reduce the fire hazard, but it would have the added benefit of maintaining native plant (and animal) diversity. One possible way to accomplish the Park Management Plan (to thin the trees) would be for the city to permit Christmas tree cutting on the mountain. A fee could be charged to administer such a program under careful controls. Whether by Christmas tree cutting, or by other innovative ways, a plan to thin the trees is needed. The vegetation of Mount Helena is at a crossroads, and today's actions or inactions will determine tomorrow's landscape on the mountain.

GEOLOGY

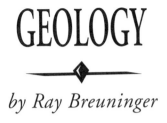

by Ray Breuninger

Geologically speaking, much of the Mount Helena we see is made up of rocks formed as sedimentary beds. Exposed in strips across the mountainside, these formations come from two different ages: Precambrian, about 1.4 billion years ago (forming the base of the mountain); and the Cambrian period, about 0.5 billion years ago, including lots of early complex lifeforms, such as trilobites. These Cambrian rocks make up the mountain's slopes and crest.

Today we can also see two major structural effects on Mount Helena's topography. The first is a syncline, or a downfold. To make a model of a syncline, take several magazines, make a trough of them, and then tip one end down to get a "plunge." On Mount Helena, the rock structure plunges southeast. The syncline can be seen best from Spring Meadow Lake, west of town. The second large geologic structure on Mount Helena is a fault, which runs north to south under the Woolston reservoirs. Don't worry; the fault is completely inactive.

What follows is a guide to some of the specific rock types on Mount Helena, along with tips for finding mineral specimens and viewing the mountain's most visible geologic features.

HELENA DOLOMITE

The Helena Dolomite provides the bedrock foundation for Mount Helena. This formation also extends north and northeast under most of suburban and downtown Helena. The Helena Dolomite is sedimentary in origin, laid down on the bed of a shallow ancient sea. In outcrops around the

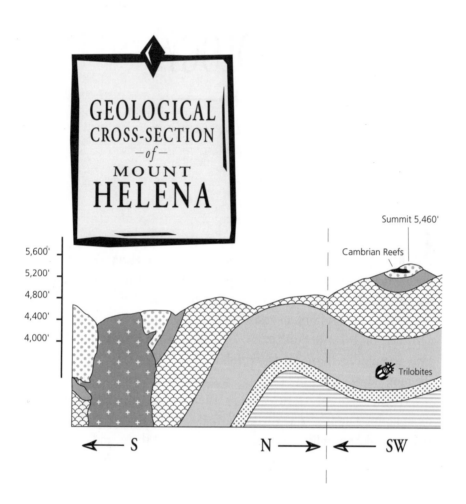

GEOLOGICAL CROSS-SECTION *of* MOUNT HELENA

Summit 5,460'

Cambrian Reefs

5,600'
5,200'
4,800'
4,400'
4,000'

Trilobites

S   N →   ← SW

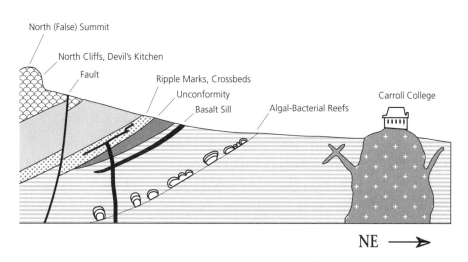

North (False) Summit

North Cliffs, Devil's Kitchen

Fault

Ripple Marks, Crossbeds

Unconformity

Basalt Sill

Algal-Bacterial Reefs

Carroll College

NE ⟶

GREAT UNCONFORMITY

EXPLANATION

Tertiary 35 my

Basalt — Sills in Helena Formation (Le Grande Cannon) and Flathead Sandstone (Reeder's Alley)

Cretaceous 80 my

Diorite, Granodiorite — Stocks of diorite porphyry in Helena Formation at Carroll College, and granodiorite in Cambrian formations in Grizzly Gulch south of Mount Helena

Cambrian 520 my

Pilgrim Limestone — Dolomitized, white and gray limestone; caps summit and southeast flank of mountain; reefs, burrows, odites

Park Shale — Dark gray to green shale, forms the saddle between the true and false (north) summits

Meagher Limestone — Mottled gray limestone, forms north cliffs; burrows, flat-pebble conglomerate, caves

Wolsey Shale — Dark gray to black, green, and reddish shale, with mica, mud cracks; on north slopes, Reeder's Alley

Flathead Sandstone — Yellow to brown and white sandstone, locally metamorphosed to quartzite; crossbedded

Precambrian 1,400 my

Snowslip Formation — Reddish shale, mud cracks

Helena Formation — Yellowish dolomite, also limestone and shale; microbial reefs (stromatolites); base not exposed

Drill holes in a big block of dolostone quarried from the Pilgrim Formations. Ray Breuninger photo.

north flank of the mountain today, you can see the formation as distinctly yellowish beds of dolostone, with a few interlayers of light-gray limestone and gray shale.

The formation dates from the Proterozoic era, about 1.4 billion years ago—it's the oldest rock in the Helena area. It is part of the Belt Supergroup of Proterozoic rocks, which extend throughout much of northwestern Montana and the Idaho Panhandle. This type of rock forms many of the high peaks in Glacier National Park and is the bedrock on Logan Pass there, where it is known as the Siyeh Formation.

The best places to see the Helena Formation close up are behind the old Eddy's Bakery building (today the Park Avenue Bakery and Miller's Crossing) just north of Reeder's Alley, and along the west end of Le Grande Cannon Boulevard, which winds along the lower slopes of Mount Helena.

Rocks formed in the early and middle part of the Proterozoic era contain no fossils save cyanobacteria, which are the so-called blue-green algae, and other similar microbes. In Deep Creek Canyon east of Townsend, single-celled animals called acritarchs have been found in the same formation, but none have been seen yet on Mount Helena. These tiny lifeforms built huge reefs of cabbage-shaped, thinly laminated structures called stromatolites. Both small and large stromatolites in reefs up to 10 feet in diameter are beautifully displayed along the north slopes of Mount Helena. The best stromatolites are just north of the park boundary, on the several little ridges above Le Grande Cannon Boulevard.

SNOWSLIP FORMATION

The Snowslip is a distinctive reddish shale, the only prominent "redbed" formation in or near Mount Helena. It forms a layer 100 to 300 feet thick, caught between the Helena Formation and the Flathead Sandstone. About

1,400 million years old, it dates from the Precambrian era and is the second oldest formation in our area.

A close look at the Snowslip shows abundant mud cracks; these indicate that the rock was formed during an era with lots of mud puddles that dried out in the sun. The red tinge to the rock comes from staining by small amounts of hematite, a common iron oxide. Redbeds usually indicate dry conditions and the presence of air with oxygen at the time of their formation.

We can develop a fairly detailed scenario for the origin of the Snowslip Formation. Picture a subtropical savannah climate, with hot, dry summers and a rainy season. Under these conditions, red, hematitic soils developed. There were no plants, no animals—only a desolate red plain, and low, eroding hills. The air contained nearly as much oxygen as it does today because of photosynthesis carried on by algae and cyanobacteria, which flourished in the nearby sea. Rain on the bare land eroded the red soil, and streams in floodstage carried the sediment to a vast delta along the edge of the Belt Sea. The mud dried, cracked under a hot sun, and slowly hardened into a red shale.

Over the next several hundred million years, the shale was gradually buried by tens of thousands of feet of younger sediments, now called the Belt Supergroup by geologists. Uplift followed burial, and slow erosion removed all the younger sediments.

By 500 million years ago, this erosion had produced another desolate plain, a lowland on which the Snowslip redbeds were exposed in a wide strip bordering a sea. The plain sank below the sea, and was flooded. A thin sheet of beach sand and pebbles was laid

Dendrites—they look like ferns or moss, but are inorganic, not fossils. They are found in the Park Shale Formation.
Ray Breuninger photo.

down as a mantle over the ancient redbeds. This beach sand hardened into rock, forming the Flathead Sandstone.

FLATHEAD SANDSTONE AND WOLSEY SHALE

The Flathead Sandstone was deposited on the bottom of a shallow tropical sea, and may include some beach sediments. It contains quartz sand and a few pebbles. Burrows and trails show that numerous animals lived on the Flathead seafloor, but we haven't found any actual fossils from the formation on Mount Helena—yet.

The Flathead formation is easily recognized by its yellow and reddish color, formed by iron oxide staining of originally white rock. It has a tendency to split into large blocks.

The point of contact between the Snowslip redbeds and the Flathead Sandstone represents a 900-million-year gap in the geologic history of our area. This vast span of time saw the evolution of multicellular life — trilobites, shellfish, crinoids, corals, and primitive vertebrates. Yet Mount Helena lacks a rock record of these events.

The best place to view the Cambrian-Precambrian contact is on the west side of the city parking lot north of Reeder's Alley and west of the Lewis and Clark Public Library. There you see the yellowish dolostone and shale beds of the Helena Formation on the north (right) extending behind nearby buildings, the reddish shale beds of the Snowslip in the middle, and the yellow/brown massive beds of Flathead Sandstone on the south (left). A thin, 3-foot sill of brownish, weathered basalt cuts through the Flathead Sandstone. Beds in all three formations are tilted down to the south at about 30 degrees.

As the Cambrian Sea deepened, the Flathead Sands were replaced by a muddy sea floor with crawling snails, worms, crustaceans, and a few trilobites. The mud hardened into the rock we now call the Wolsey Shale. This formation underlies many of the mountain's grass-covered, dry slopes, just above the Flathead Sandstone. Only one trilobite has been found on Mount Helena to date.

MEAGHER LIMESTONE AND PARK SHALE

The Meagher Limestone forms Mount Helena's most striking geologic

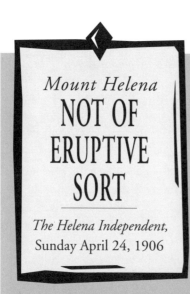

Mount Helena
NOT OF ERUPTIVE SORT

The Helena Independent,
Sunday April 24, 1906

An idle and silly rumor which a child of six could start, was enough yesterday to send some women and more children into hysterics. How the rumor started no one knows, but it rapidly spread and was the principal topic of conversation on the streets yesterday. The "mind of the mob" held full sway. Children passed it from one to another at school and they in turn passed it on to their parents. Some laughed at it while others took it seriously. Children came home from school screaming with terror; Mount Helena was going to erupt to-day; and the millenium had come. Thus said the children; the older ones repeated it to the smaller children, delighting in the spectacle of fear they had aroused. Then the tale gathered momentum and grew and spread and the sky became overcast with the size of it.

GROWS IN TELLING

First, it was only Mount Helena and then some one added Mount Ascension, and then crossed the valley and took in Bear Tooth and then Old Baldy down near Townsend. It was amusing. Because some one who knows no more about what is going on in the bowels of the earth than they do about their own business told a silly tale to fill in the gaps of conversation some people believed it. To lend weight to the story. It was added that Tatum had predicted it and then they added that McIvar-Tyndall had also said so. Forsooth it must be true. To frighten the people still more, some persons proposed to get some red tire and giant powder and set it off on Mount Helena. This may still be done to-day.

MOUNTAIN NOT VOLCANIC

As a matter of fact, scientists who have made a lifelong study of volcanos have declared that this portion of Montana is not volcanic, never was and never will be. It is of an entirely different formation and not of igneous origin.

The story spread yesterday was the same as the one that went the rounds of the country 25 years ago. Some one declared the world was coming to an end in 1881. Many persons believed it. ♦

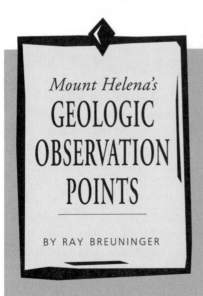

Mount Helena's
GEOLOGIC
OBSERVATION
POINTS

BY RAY BREUNINGER

Here are some of Mount Helena's most outstanding geologic sites.

REEDER'S ALLEY

A good place to view the Flathead Sandstone-Wolsey Shale contact. Ripple marks and crossbedding are exposed in Flathead Sandstone beds just to the right of the Stonehouse Restaurant. Farther up the gulch, near the Morelli Bridge, are good outcrops of Wolsey Shale, which is burrowed and has lots of mica flecks. Geologic history suggests these beds should contain trilobites.

MOUNT HELENA PARKING LOT

The lot is bordered with boulders of Flathead Sandstone and Meagher Limestone. Look for crossbedding in the Flathead, and orangeish burrow mottling in the gray Meagher.

PROSPECT SHAFTS

The rocks and minerals in the old prospect pits along the east ridge tell an interesting, multistaged geologic story. In the first stage, the bedrock —which is white Pilgrim dolostone —was shattered by motion along several faults. Some of the rock remained as angular, broken pieces, while some was completely crushed to powder. Then hot water (or perhaps superheated steam) seeped along the faults, and enveloped the rock fragments. Various minerals crystallized out from the hot breccia. Finally, the breccia was soaked with shallow, oxygenated groundwater and some of its minerals were changed to new, low-temperature forms.

Limonite is the generic term for the yellowish to rusty-colored masses of iron oxides seen throughout Montana's mining districts. It is also called "iron hat" or gossan. On Mount Helena, it occurs in fractured rock along faults and mineralized zones. The limonite fault breccias contain yellow jasper, white agate, bright green malachite, pyrite (fool's gold) and, maybe, a little real gold. Rockhounds have also reported lead minerals here, including shiny, silver-gray galena and white hemimorphite.

DEVIL'S KITCHEN
This cave was sliced open by erosion in the Meagher Limestone. Several other small caves are in these cliffs, popular with climbers.

SUMMIT
Massive dolostone beds jut out on the narrow summit ridge of Mount Helena. The dolostone resists erosion and is worn away only slowly by wind and water. The lower slopes of the mountain are formed of soft shale which erodes rapidly, undercutting and steepening the summit slopes.

Look for peculiar white mottles in the dark gray dolostone (which is part of the Pilgrim Limestone). These mottles are the traces of burrowing animals that lived in the shallow Cambrian sea about 520 million years ago.

TALC MINE
Soft, white talc comes from a vein cutting through dolostone in the Pilgrim Limestone exposed on the southeast foot of the mountain. It's pure enough to make talcum powder. A few tons of talc were once mined from the vein and shipped out by rail. The talc is interlaced with white dolomite crystals.

The easiest place to see the talc is in a mine dump and old adit to the vein at the south side of the small dolostone quarry above the lime kilns near the mouth of Grizzly Gulch. This is on private land, so ask permission before collecting. The adit was recently gated off as part of the State of Montana's abandoned mine reclamation program. The talc vein is 1 to 4 feet thick, and is exposed in steep, dangerous cliffs near the top of the quarry. ♦

feature: the prominent cliffs just below the summit on the mountain's north side. The formation has provided beautiful bluestone, blue and gold limestone, and Helena marble. This fine building stone was quarried at various sites along the south side of town, although the formation was not quarried within the current boundaries of Mount Helena park. Although it forms massive cliffs, the limestone is mostly thin bedded and extensively burrowed. Some beds contain abundant trilobite shell fragments.

Park Shale.
Ray Breuninger photo.

The Park Shale is a drab, olive-gray colored shale which lies on top of the Meagher Limestone. It is soft and erodes to form gentle slopes. Look for chips of Park Shale in the saddle between the two summits of Mount Helena. The shale was deposited as mud in a shallow Cambrian sea, and contains the delicate shells of a few tiny inarticulate brachiopods. These inconspicuous fossils are about half an inch in diameter. The geologic map show several sites where the brachiopods are found.

PILGRIM LIMESTONE

In the Helena area, the Pilgrim Limestone is entirely altered to dolostone—a limestone that got soaked in brine and altered to the mineral dolomite. The dark gray dolostone here retains the original bedding of the limestone, and is dotted with peculiar white mottles formed by burrowing animals such as brachiopods, crustaceans, or perhaps worms. The Pilgrim Formation is a marine deposit of Upper Cambrian age, about 520 million years old.

While making his 1963 geologic map of the Helena area, Adolph Knopf was impressed by the extensive dolomitization of the Pilgrim Limestone near Helena, and classified the formation as Hasmark Dolomite. The Hasmark is a massive dolostone formation in the Philipsburg area. This is a good example of how a rigid classification of a natural feature doesn't quite fit nature's complexity—the Helena area dolostone actually sits squarely on the boundary between the Pilgrim Limestone on the east and the Hasmark Formation on the west.

With abundant oolites (limestone pellets about $1/16$ inch in diameter), reefs of microbial origin, and trace fossils, the burrowed Pilgrim Limestone is the youngest and highest of Mount Helena's Cambrian formations. The summit and entire southeastern ridge of the mountain are formed of this rock.

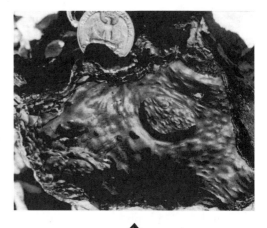

Slag—melted rock from a lime kiln.
Ray Breuninger photo.

MINERALS AND MINES

Faults on Mount Helena's northeast side, though no longer active, are related to the igneous activity that created the Boulder Batholith, a giant intrusion of granite just 3 miles south, near Unionville. The faults are also associated with the Helena area's gold mineralization. Look for the Prospect Shafts mine holes and adits dug by early Helena miners on the east side of the mountain. One adit ran completely through the ridge of Flathead Sandstone above Reeder's Alley.

During the mining era, Mount Helena was also the site of several lime kilns, which produced lime by heating limestone and dolostone. Look for white calcined fragments around kiln ruins or dumps. The mountain was also logged in earlier days—for the lime kilns, charcoal production, and timber needed for local mine braces and railroad ties.

THE VIEW FROM THE SUMMIT

Visitors to the summit of Mount Helena can get a good sampling of the geologic history of the Helena area. Here's a quick look at the surrounding landscapes:

The Helena Bench. Helena lies directly below the northeast slopes of the mountain. The city is built on a north-facing pediment—a gently sloping erosion surface which truncates the steeply tilted bedrock. A thin layer of gold-bearing bouldery gravel conceals the ancient bedrock, the 1.4-billion-year-old Helena Formation.

The South Hills. These forested ridges are formed of a thick series of Paleozoic sedimentary rocks, which were originally laid down as more-or-less-horizontal beds in an equatorial sea. When the Rocky Mountains formed, these rocks were uplifted, then tilted down and to the south, so that as you drive up any one of the gulches south of town you step up in time, beginning with Cambrian rocks (as on Mount Helena) and climbing into younger, oil-rich Jefferson Dolostone, fossil-filled Three Forks Shale, and the Madison Limestone, high on Mount Ascension.

Unionville and Points South. South of Mount Helena, the view includes densely forested peaks and valleys. The Paleozoic formations of the South Hills loop through theses hills like waving stripes on a flag, but are cut off abruptly by a mass of igneous rock—the Boulder Batholith. The batholith extends from this, its northern edge, over an immense area that reaches south past Butte. Patches of volcanic rocks and hardened volcanic ash and breccia cap some of the high points. For instance, far to the southwest, look for a pinkish tinge on the bare rock capping Colorado Peak. This is the eroded remnant of a rhyolite lava flow.

The Helena Valley Fault. Along the base of the North Hills is a sharply defined boundary between lodgepole pine forest and open sage grass and prairie. This vegetative pattern traces a major strike-slip fault, with a horizontal offset of perhaps 10 or more miles. Fortunately, the fault is not very active at the present time, and poses little earthquake risk.

About where Lake Helena is today, the northeast corner of the valley has dropped down along the Helena Valley Fault—by several thousand feet. At the same time, the valley side of the fault has shifted westward, widening the valley horizontally. Another fault, the Iron Gulch Fault (or Scratchgravel Hills Fault) bounds the valley on its west side, roughly parallel to Green Meadow Road. This fault is potentially active.

Spring Meadow Lake. This manmade lake occupies an old gravel quarry north of Mount Helena. The gravel was deposited by torrential floodwaters from melting glaciers along and near the Continental Divide up Tenmile Creek. Much of the Helena Valley was filled by such gravel, along with a lot of sand and mud. This material forms the bottomland of the valley, and holds a vast reservoir of shallow groundwater.

Small glaciers formed during a succession of ice ages put the final touches on our high-country scenery. All the mountain ranges on the skyline —except the North Hills and Scratchgravel Hills—hosted alpine glaciers, some as recently as 11,000 years ago.

The Boulder Batholith. The north edge of this great batholith lies in Unionville, only a few miles south of Mount Helena. Several small granitic "satellite" intrusions are closer still—one tiny intrusion is a half mile up Grizzly Gulch and another lies within Helena city limits east of the mountain, concealed under houses, yards, and pavement near Dry Gulch. The batholith's tough igneous rock is granite (quartz monzonite). It contains tightly interlocked grains of quartz and two feldspars (orthoclase and plagioclase). Black grains are mostly biotite mica and hornblende; a closer look shows some pyrite and yellowish zircon. You can see granite in the building stones in the parking lot of Reeder's Alley, and in the bouldery gravel along the bottom of Grizzly Gulch. Most of the block granite was quarried from sites (now abandoned) on MacDonald Pass, south of Unionville, or near Clancy.

MOUNT HELENA
—and—
ROCK-HOUNDING ETIQUETTE

BY RAY BREUNINGER

Should the city permit rock-hounding on Mount Helena? This is a tricky question. Mount Helena offers a virtually inexhaustible supply of nice rock specimens, notably limestone, dolostone, shale, and sandstone. There is no reason why you shouldn't pick up a few samples, especially if you are making a local rock collection. This directly serves the educational purpose of the park.

On the other hand, most minerals and fossils on the mountain are strictly limited in quantity and occurrence. For instance, you can find chips of the green copper mineral malachite at only a few places near the Prospect Shafts Trail. If even a few of the many hikers collect malachite, within a few tens of years the prospect pits will be picked clean. While malachite is by no means rare yet, it is better left in place as a memento of the early mining history of the area, and as a geological specimen for all who have the energy to climb onto the mountain's eastern slopes.

OTHER RECOMMENDATIONS FOR ROCKHOUNDING:

- Feel free to collect a few interesting samples if it's for a good purpose—your rock collection, or a gift for a child. Collect only loose pieces.

- Leave fossils and minerals in place for all to see.

- Don't damage natural bedrock outcrops—no hammering, chiseling, or prying to free specimens from an outcrop.

- Ask permission to collect on private land bordering Mount Helena Park.

- Don't roll or throw rocks down the mountain or onto a trail. ♦

RECREATION

◆───

For more than 125 years, Mount Helena has been explored by Helena's residents and visitors. For more than ninety years, it has been the cornerstone of the city's park system. It is a special and magical place, and will remain so only if we take pains to preserve it. In 1995, the City of Helena developed a park management plan designed to help guide the use of this special city park, emphasizing the maintenance of the natural setting. The philosophy of the plan reflects the special relationship between the park and the community.

> The Park will be managed for the enjoyment of the citizens of Helena, in a manner that maintains and enhances its natural character. The Park will be managed to accommodate the gradual increase in use that is expected to occur as the City grows. . . . The City will continue to work with citizen volunteers and organizations who will provide ongoing responsibility for trail maintenance. Increased community support, in the form of donations of labor and money, will be actively solicited.

For most of the park's history, civic efforts have provided for maintenance and land acquisition. A significant part of the park's acreage was acquired between 1903 and 1911, but only one trail was constructed during that time. Between 1973 and 1975, seven more trails were created in the park; two more trails joined the mountain system in 1995. The more than 700 acres of land that make up the current city park are now accessible by ten trails, reaching all sections. A walk or ride on any of them will expose you to this beautiful and unusual city park and its wonderful features.

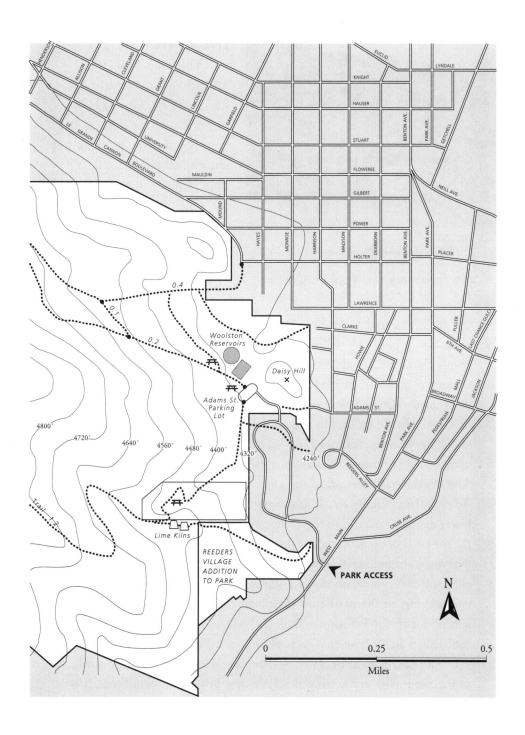

THE TRAILS

The 1906 Trail (1903)—
The 1906 Trail, actually constructed in 1903 by the Helena Improvement Society, is the most popular trail to the summit of Mount Helena. The Improvement Society planned the trail on an easy grade, ensuring that more of Helena's citizens could experience the climb. From 1904 to the 1930s, a gazebo gracing the top of the mountain could be reached via

Adams Street parking lot. Wayne Phillips photo

the trail. The trail is 1.6 miles long and gains more than 1,000 feet in elevation. It passes by the limestone cliffs and Devil's Kitchen Cave, and winds through a stand of trees that was planted in 1906. It also crosses under the area that burned in a 1973 fire. In 1979, the 1906 trail was designated a national recreational trail as a part of the Forest Service's Ridge Trail—the first local trail in Montana to receive such recognition.

The Prairie Trail (1973)—The Prairie Trail was the first trail constructed in a flurry of activity that began on the mountain in the 1970s. The Prairie Trail veers off of the 1906 trail less than 1,000 feet from the Adams Street parking lot. It winds around the north face of the mountain lower than, but parallel to the 1906 trail, turning south and cutting across the west side of the mountain. The trail is named for the prairie wildflowers that you will see along its length, but you also get great views of the limestone cliffs and of the varied north-slope vegetation. A Douglas-fir forest is rapidly encroaching on the prairie on the north slope. When you approach the junction with the Panhandle Trail, you will be very near Bitterroot Point (also called Sunset Point), a great place to see the state flower.

The East Side Trail (1974)—The East Side trail crosses the east face of the mountain, connecting the 1906 and Prospect Shafts Trails. It is a fairly level trail that passes right above the "H."

The Back Side Trail (1974)—This trail crosses the southwest corner of the park. It is relatively easy, crossing through grassy ponderosa pine woodlands. It connects the Prospect Shafts Trail with the West End and Prairie trails, making for a nice loop around the mountain.

The Prospect Shafts Trail (1974)—This trail is named for the deep prospect shafts possibly left by a mining company in the 1880s which are located along its length. It takes you through a variety of landscapes on the south side of the mountain. When the trail was built, the shafts were sealed.

The West End Trail (1974)—Located in the remote southwest corner of the park, this trail leads through a meadow in the saddle between Mount Helena and the next mountain in the ridge. It links the 1906 Trail and the Forest Service's Ridge Trail, forming the Mount Helena Ridge National Recreational Trail. It is a pleasant 6 miles to Park City from the border.

The Hogback Trail (1974)—From the summit to the Prospect Shafts Trail, this trail follows the Hogback Ridge. This trail is steep and rocky and is a lot more fun going down than going up. However, it offers great views.

The North Access Trail (1975)—This trail connects North Side residents with the park. It comes from the subdivision above Le Grande Cannon and heads up into the park through the prairie/Douglas-fir forest-in- transition.

The Panhandle Trail (1995)—This trail also connects the north side of Helena to the mountain. It starts above Le Grande Cannon, heads south into the park, and connects with the Quartzite Trail, also constructed in 1995. These trails provide the first real north access into the park.

The Quartzite Trail (1995)—The Quartzite Trail cuts across the north side of the park and heads toward Bitteroot/Sunset Point where it connects with the Prairie Trail.

RECREATION ON THE MOUNTAIN

Hikers, joggers, walkers, skiers, mountain bikers, picnickers, bird and wildlife watchers, clubs, classes, and dog walkers all visit Mount Helena. The trails on the mountain see a great deal of use, particularly during the summer months. The City of Helena recognizes this and has tried to accommodate all of the potential recreation opportunities on the mountain.

A family hike to the summit. Nathanael Greene photo.

There is remarkably little conflict between different activities, and in its 1995 management plan the city has declared,

> The whole range of outdoor recreational activities is to be allowed in Mount Helena Park, except those involving firearms, motorized vehicles, or those which would result in a lasting and significant change in the Park's existing semi-natural environment. Mount Helena will always be a wildland-open space park. . . .

Rules and recommendations for park use are posted at the Adams Street parking lot. These are designed to increase everyone's access to our remarkable park.

The city has also declared that it will increase access for the elderly and the disabled in the spirit that Mount Helena should be everyone's park. Some areas of the park have been set aside for additional development with this thought in mind.

Mount Helena
PARK RULES
—and—
ETIQUETTE

Mount Helena is a unique and fragile resource that provides a wide variety of recreational opportunities. To ensure an enjoyable experience for all visitors, and to maintain the park's natural condition, the City of Helena asks that you observe the following park rules and etiquette.

PROHIBITED:
- Recreational fires, horses, camping, hunting, motor vehicles;
- Dogs must be within sight of the owner and under control;
- Dog excrement must be removed by the owner;
- No littering: all trash must be packed out;
- All trail users yield to the uphill user, faster users yield to slower users until it is safe to pass;
- Stay off any erosion areas or trails marked closed.

BIKES:
- Always ride under control, yield to uphill and all slower users;
- Stay on trails;
- Slow or walk bike when approaching blind corners and narrow trails;
- Do not lock brakes or skid tires when descending;
- No bike riding when trails are wet.

ETIQUETTE:
- Use common courtesy. Be aware that hikers, small children, dog owners, joggers, and mountain bikers share the Park's trails.
- Avoid disturbing wildlife and going off-trail, especially straight-up or down.
- Avoid use when trails are wet.

RECOMMENDED BIKE USE:
Ascent: (1) 1906 Trail, (2) Prospect Shafts Trail, (3) Back Side Trail
Descent: (1) Back Side Trail, (2) Prospect Shafts Trail, (3) Prairie Trail
- The 1906 Trail is the primary route hikers take to the summit; bikers should not use this trail to descend. Bikers should avoid riding during busy hiking periods (weekend days) and riding in large groups.

Enjoyment and maintenance of the park depends on park visitors. Please help the City of Helena by reporting vandalism, motor-vehicle use, or other prohibited use, and making any suggestions or complaints to the Parks Department at 447-8463. ◆

Mount Helena
PROCESSION
— of —
COLOR

BY BONNIE HEIDEL

Regular visitors to Mount Helena will notice the park's vibrant procession of color. The following calendar of events may help you identify the mountain's wild plants on your next visit.

FEBRUARY

Sap flow starts in deciduous trees and shrubs during warm weather, swelling the buds of serviceberry, mountain maple, and other woody plants. In mild winters, bitterbrush timidly puts out its first set of leaves for the year.

LATE MARCH/EARLY APRIL

Easter daisy flowers, Douglasia, and fuzzy buds of pasqueflower emerge.

MID-APRIL/EARLY MAY

Lavender, pink, and yellow adorn the hillsides heralding spring with pasqueflower, phlox, shooting stars, fritillary, kittentails, leafy musineon, and nine-leaf lomatium.

MID-MAY

Hillsides turn into constellations, with many tiny four- and five-petaled white flowers of thread-leaved sandwort, field chickweed, and rockcress.

Bright new splashes of color appear. Rock-hugging cushion plants adorn rocky benches and knolls with intense sky blue (forget-me-not), gold (cushion goldenweed), and violet (rabbit's-foot locoweed). The flowering plants tend to be taller than this starting lineup as the season progresses.

The first shrubs to display flowers include squaw currant and golden currant.

LATE MAY

In mild years, this is the time of greatest color and combinations of color. By the end of May, nearly half of the two hundred plus flowering plant species on Mount Helena will have started (if not finished) their flowering. Attention-getters along the trails include white coiled-beak, old man's whiskers, penstemons, and yellow gromwell. Showy flowers begin to appear on shrubs such as serviceberry, chokecherry, and mock-orange. This is also some of the busiest flowering time for grasses and grasslike plants whose flowers are anything but showy, pollinated by the wind instead of insects.

EARLY JUNE/MID-JUNE
Arrowleaf balsamroot always puts on a striking show. Since the mid-1980s, this plant has had a hard time vying with Dalmatian toadflax. Bitterroot is uncommon but puts out a glorious flower.

LATE JUNE/EARLY JULY
Blanket flower and sego lily join the company of wild roses for an extravagant combination of colors. Some plants are more conspicuous after flowering than during it—these include old man's whiskers and ground plum.

JULY/EARLY AUGUST
By now the desertlike plants such as prickly pear cactus and lesser rushy milkvetch have gone into flower, as have the forest plants of the deep shade. Dotted blazing star lends its color to rich-textured grassy hillsides that are often dry by this time of year.

LATE AUGUST/SEPTEMBER
Sagebrush, rabbitbrush, and goldenrod usually have the flowering scene to themselves at the end of the summer. But sometimes the effects of extra moisture and shorter day-length will reactivate a few early blooming plants when the temperatures turn cool again. Harebell will often come back for an encore. Look for the "fruits" of the season—rose hips, juniper berries, seedheads on grasses, and all the second-year pine cones ready to carry wildlife through the winter and generate new plants on the mountain. ♦

SELECTED REFERENCES

REFERENCES—GEOLOGY

Breuninger, Ray H., and John Childs. *Guidebook of the Helena Area*. Montana Bureau of Mines and Geology Special Publication 95. 1987

Knopf, Adolph. *Ore Deposits of the Helena Mining Region, Montana*. U.S. Geological Survey Bulletin 527. 1913.

_____, *Geology of the Northern Part of the Boulder Bathylith and Adjacent Area, Montana*. U.S. Geological Survey Miscellaneous Geologic Investigations Map I-381. 1963.

McClernan, Henry G. *Metallic Mineral Deposits of Lewis and Clark County, Montana*. Montana Bureau of Mines and Geology Memoir No. 52. 1983.

Stickney, Michael C. *Quarternary Geologic Map of the Helena Valley, Montana*. Montana Bureau of Mines and Geology Geologic Map Series No. 46. 1987.

REFERENCES—PLANT AND PLANT COMMUNITIES

Dorn, R. D. *Vascular plants of Montana*. Mountain West Publishing, Cheyenne, WY. 1984.

Hitchcock, C. L., and A. Cronquist. *Flora of the Pacific Northwest*. University of Washington Press, Seattle. 1973.

REFERENCES—BUGS AND BUTTERFLIES

Several books may assist butterfly watchers as they wander around the park. A good book for a casual observer or beginner is the *Golden Guide to Butterflies and Moths*. Much more complete, and a bit more difficult to use, are *The Audubon Society Field Guide to North American Butterflies* by Robert Michael Pyle, and the *Handbook for Butterfly Watchers*, also by Pyle. All three books can be found at the Lewis and Clark Public Library.

REFERENCES—HISTORY

The Montana Historical Society collection of materials preserved by the Helena Improvement Society, including many articles from the *Helena Independent* and the *Montana Standard*. The *Helena Independent Record, Helena Monthly, Helena, an Illustrated History* by Vivian Palladin and Jean Baucus, *Gold in the Gulch,* by Jean Baucus, and the document of nomination for recognition of Mount Helena in the National Register of Historic Places by Ellen Sievert were extremely helpful in putting together the history of Mount Helena's improvement.

APPENDIX

Animal, Plant, & Mineral Lists

MOUNT HELENA WILDLIFE LIST

Common Name	Scientific Name	Occurrence Sp	Su	F	W
AMPHIBIANS					
Long-toed salamander	*Ambystoma macrodactylum*	/	/	/	/
Boreal (Western) toad	*Bufo boreas*	/	/	/	/
REPTILES					
Rubber boa	*Charina bottae*	/	/	/	/
Racer	*Coluber constrictor*	/	/	/	/
Gopher snake	*Pituophis catenfir*	X	X	X	X
Western rattlesnake	*Crotalus viridis*	/	/	/	/
Common garter snake	*Thamnophis sirtalis*	/	/	/	/
Western garter snake	*Thamnophis elegans*	X	X	X	X
MAMMALS					
SHREWS					
Masked shrew	*Sorex cinereus*	/	/	/	/
Montane shrew	*Sorex monicola*	X	X	X	X
BATS					
Little brown bat	*Myotis lucifugus*	X	X	X	X
Big brown bat	*Eptesicus fuscus*	X	X	X	X
Hoary bat	*Nycteris cinerea*	X	X	X	X
RABBITS, HARES					
Mountain cottontail	*Sylvilagus nuttallii*	X	X	X	X
Snowshoe hare	*Lepus americanus*	X	X	X	X

Sp = Spring, Su = Summer, F = Fall, W = Winter
X = likely to occur on Mount Helena or the Ridge sometime during this season
/ = possibly occurs on Mount Helena or the Ridge during this season
Mount Helena Ridge is defined as extending from the City Park to Park City, to the south.

Common Name	Scientific Name	Occurrence			
		Sp	Su	F	W
RODENTS					
Yellow-pine chipmunk	*Eutamias amoenus*	X	X	X	X
Red-tailed chipmunk	*Eutamias ruficaudus*	/	/	/	/
Yellow-bellied marmot	*Marmota flaviventris*	/	/	/	/
Columbian ground squirrel	*Spermophilus columbianus*	X	X	X	X
Golden-mantled grnd squirrel	*Spermophilus lateralis*	X	X	X	X
Red squirrel	*Tamiasciurus hudsonicus*	X	X	X	X
Northern flying squirrel	*Glaucomys sabrinus*	/	/	/	/
Northern pocket gopher	*Thomomys talpoides*	X	X	X	X
Deer mouse	*Peromyscus maniculatus*	X	X	X	X
Bushy-tailed woodrat	*Neotoma cinerea*	X	X	X	X
Gapper's red-backed vole	*Clethrionomys gapperi*	X	X	X	X
Meadow vole	*Microtus pennsylvanicus*	X	X	X	X
Montane vole	*Microtus montanus*	/	/	/	/
Long-tailed vole	*Microtus longicaudus*	/	/	/	/
Porcupine	*Erethizon dorsatum*	X	X	X	X
PREDATORS					
Coyote	*Canis latrans*	X	X	X	X
Gray wolf	*Canis lupus*			/	
Red fox	*Vulpes vulpes*	X	X	X	X
Black bear	*Ursus americanus*	X	X	X	X
Long-tailed weasel	*Mustela frenata*	X	X	X	X
Wolverine	*Gulo gulo*	/			/
Badger	*Taxidea taxus*	X	X	X	X
Striped skunk	*Mephitis mephitis*	X	X	X	X
Mountain lion	*Felis concolor*	X	X	X	X
Bobcat	*Lynx rufus*	X	X	X	X
UNGULATES					
Mule deer	*Odocoileus hemionus*	X	X	X	X
White-tailed deer	*Odocoileus virginianus*	X	X		X
Elk	*Cervus elaphus*	X	X	X	X
Moose	*Alces alces*	X	X	X	X

Sp = Spring, Su = Summer, F = Fall, W = Winter

X = likely to occur on Mount Helena or the Ridge sometime during this season

/ = possibly occurs on Mount Helena or the Ridge during this season

Mount Helena Ridge is defined as extending from the City Park to Park City, to the south.

MOUNT HELENA BIRD LIST

Species	Abundance	Resident/Breeding Status
Turkey vulture	uc	t,s
Red-tailed hawk	uc	t,s
Merlin	uc	r
Prairie falcon	r	rB
Blue grouse	uc	rB
Mourning dove	uc	sB
Northern pygmy owl	uc	rB
Calliope hummingbird	uc	sB
Rufous hummingbird	uc	sB
Downy woodpecker	uc	r
Hairy woodpecker	uc	r
Northern flicker	uc	r
Western wood-pewee	r	s
Hammond's flycatcher	uc	sB
Dusky flycatcher	uc	sB
Gray jay	r	t,w
Stellar's jay	r	t,w
Clark's nutcracker	uc	r
Black-billed magpie	uc	r
American crow	r	s
Raven	uc	rB
Black-capped chickadee	uc	rB
Mountain chickadee	c	rB
red-breasted nuthatch	c	rB
White-breasted nuthatch	uc	rB
Rock wren	c	sB
Golden-crowned kinglet	c	rB
ruby-crowned kinglet	r	sB
mountain bluebird	c	sB
Townsend's solitaire	c	rB
Hermit thrush	c	sB
American robin	c	sB
Bohemian waxwing	uc	t,w
Cedar waxwing	uc	sB
Solitary vireo	uc	sB
Yellow warbler	uc	sB
Yellow-rumped warbler	c	sB

Abundance: r = rare, uc = uncommon, c = common
Resident status: t = transient, s = summer, r = resident, w = winter
Breeding status: B = breeding or suspected breeding

Species	Abundance	Resident/Breeding Status
Western tanager	uc	sB
Lazuli bunting	uc	sB
Green-tailed towhee	c	sB
Spotted towhee	c	sB
Chipping sparrow	c	sB
Vesper sparrow	c	sB
Lark sparrow	r	sB
White-crowned sparrow	uc	t
Dark-eyed junco	c	sB
Western meadowlark	c	sB
Brewer's blackbird	r	sB
Rosy finch	r	t,w
Cassin's finch	uc	rB
House finch	r	r
Red crossbill	uc	t
Pine siskin	uc	rB
American goldfinch	uc	sB

Abundance r - rare, uc-uncommon, c-common
Resident status: t-transient, s-summer, r - resident, w - winter
Breeding status: B- breeding or suspected breeding

MOUNT HELENA PLANT LIST

TREES AND SHRUBS

Scientific Name	Common Name	G	R	T	F	Family
Acer glabrum	Mountain maple	-	-	C	U	Maple
Amelanchier alnifolia	Western serviceberry	U	U	C	U	Rose
Arctostaphylos uva-ursi	Bearberry	-	-	U	U	Heath
Artemisia cana	Silver sage	U	-	U	-	Aster
Artemisia tridentata ssp. *vaseyana*	Big sage	U	-	-	-	Aster
Berberis repens	Creeping Oregon grape	-	-	U	U	Barberry
Chrysothamnus nauseosus	Common rabbitbrush	C	U	U	-	Aster
Chrysothamnus viscidifl.	Green rabbitbrush	U	-	-	-	Aster
Juniperus communis	Common juniper	-	U	U	C	Juniper
Juniperus scopulorum	Rocky Mountain juniper	-	U	U	C	Juniper
Lonicera tartarica*	Tartarian honeysuckle	-	-	U	-	Honeysuckle
Philadelphus lewisii	Mock orange	-	-	C	-	Mock orange
Physocarpus malvaceus	Mallow ninebark	-	-	-	U	Rose
Pinus contorta	Lodgepole pine	-	-	-	C	Pine
Pinus flexilis	Limber pine	-	U	-	U	Pine
Pinus ponderosa	Ponderosa pine	U	U	U	C	Pine
Potentilla fruticosa	Shubby cinquefoil	-	-	U	U	Rose
Prunus virginiana	Chokecherry	U	-	C	U	Rose
Pseudotsuga menziesii	Douglas fir	C	-	U	C	Pine
Purshia tridentata	Bitterbrush	C	U	C	C	Rose
Rhus trilobata	Skunkbush sumac	U	U	C	U	Sumac
Ribes aureum	Golden currant	U	U	C	U	Gooseberry
Ribes cereum	Squaw currant	U	U	C	U	Gooseberry
Ribes viscosissimum	Sticky currant	-	-	U	U	Gooseberry
Rosa arkansana	Prairie rose	C	-	U	-	Rose
Rosa woodsii	Woods rose	U	U	C	U	Rose
Rubus parviflora	Thimbleberry	-	-	-	U	Rose
Sambucus racemosa	Elderberry	-	-	U	-	Honeysuckle
Shepherdia canadensis	Canada buffaloberry	-	-	U	C	Oleaster
Sorbus domestica*	Mountain ash	-	U	-	-	Rose
Spiraea betulifolia	Shiny-leaf spiraea	-	-	-	U	Rose
Symphoricarpos albus	Western snowberry	-	-	-	U	Honeysuckle
Symphoricarpos occidentalis	Mountain snowberry	-	-	C	-	Honeysuckle
Tetradymia canescens	Gray horsebrush	C	U	U	U	Aster

* = non-native   **G** = grassland and shrubland   **T** = tall shrub draws
C = common   **R** = cliff and rock outcrops   **F** = forest and woodland
U = uncommon

WILDFLOWERS AND FERNS

Scientific Name	Common Name	G	R	T	F	Family
Achillea millefolium	Yarrow	C	U	C	U	Aster
Agastache urticifolia	Nettle-leaf giant-hyssop	U	-	U	-	Mint
Agoseris glauca	Pale agoseris/ Mountain dandelion	U	-	-	-	Aster
Allium cernuum	Nodding onion	C	-	U	U	Lily
Alyssum desertorum*	Desert alyssum	C	C	-	-	Mustard
Amaranthus albus	Pigweed	-	-	U	-	Pigweed
Anemone cylindrica	Candle anemone	U	-	-	U	Buttercup
Anemone multifida	Cliff anemone	-	-	-	U	Buttercup
Anemone patens	Pasqueflower	C	-	C	U	Buttercup
Antennaria dimorpha	Low pussytoes	C	-	U	-	Aster
Antennaria microphylla	Rosy pussytoes	C	U	U	U	Aster
Antennaria neglecta	Field pussytoes	-	-	-	U	Aster
Antennaria umbrinella	Umber pussytoes	U	U	-	-	Aster
Apocynum androsaemifolium	Spreading dogbane	U	-	-	U	Dogbane
Arabis holboellii	Holboell's rockcress	U	-	-	-	Mustard
Arabis microphylla	Littleleaf rockcress	C	-	U	-	Mustard
Arenaria capillaris	Thread-leaved sandwort	C	-	-	-	Pink
Arnica cordifolia	Heart-leaved arnica	-	-	U	U	Aster
Arnica sororia	Twin arnica	U	-	U	-	Aster
Artemisia biennis	Biennial wormwood	-	U	-		Aster
Artemisia dracunculus	Tarragon	U	-	U	-	Aster
Artemisia frigida	Fringed sage	C	U	-	-	Aster
Artemisia ludoviciana	Prairie sagewort/ White sage	U	-	-	-	Aster
Asparagus officinalis*	Asparagus	-	-	U	-	Lily
Aster chilensis	Long-leaved aster	U	-	U	-	Aster
Aster conspicuous	Showy aster	-	-	U	C	Aster
Astragalus adsurgens	Standing milkvetch	C	-	-	-	Bean
Astragalus convallarius	Lesser rushy milkvetch	U	-	-	U	Bean
Astragalus gilviflorus	Plains orophaca/ Tufted milkvetch	U	C	-	-	Bean
Astragalus gracilis	Slender milkvetch	C	-	-	-	Bean
Astragalus miser	Weedy milkvetch	-	-	U	U	Bean
Astragalus missouriensis	Missouri milkvetch	U	-	-	-	Bean
Astragarus crassicarpus	Ground plum	-	-	U	-	Bean
Balsamorhiza sagittata	Arrowleaf balsamroot	C	-	U	C	Aster
Besseya wyomingensis	Wyoming kittentails	C	-	-	U	Figwort

* = non-native   **G** = grassland and shrubland   **T** = tall shrub draws
C = common   **R** = cliff and rock outcrops   **F** = forest and woodland
U = uncommon

Scientific Name	Common Name	G	R	T	F	Family
Calochortus nuttallii	Sego lily	C	-	-	-	Lily
*Camelina microcarpa**	False flax	C	U	C	-	Mustard
*Camelina sativa**	Gold-of-pleasure	U	-	U	-	Mustard
Campanula rotundifolia	Harebell	C	U	U	U	Harebell
*Cardaria draba**	Hoary pepperwort	U	-	U	-	Mustard
*Carduus nutans**	Musk thistle	U	-	U	-	Aster
Castilleja pallescens	Salish indian paintbrush	C	-	-	-	Figwort
*Centaurea diffusa**	Tumble knapweed	U	-	-	-	Aster
*Centaurea maculosa**	Spotted knapweed	U	-	U	-	Aster
Cerastium arvense	Field chickweed	C	-	C	-	Pink
Chaenactis douglasii	Hoary chaenactis	U	-	-	-	Aster
Cheilanthes feei	Lip-fern	-	U	-	-	Fern
*Chenopodium album**	Lambsquarter	U	-	U	-	Goosefoot
Chenopodium leptophyllum	Slimleaf goosefoot	U	U	-	-	Goosefoot
Chrysopsis villosa	Hairy golden-aster	C	U	-	U	Aster
*Cirsium arvense**	Canada thistle	-	-	U	-	Aster
Cirsium undulatum	Wavy-leaved thistle	C	-	U	U	Aster
Clematis columbiana	Columbia clematis	U	C	-	U	Buttercup
Clematis hirsutissima	Vaseflower clematis/ Sugar bowl	U	-	U	-	Buttercup
Clematis ligusticifolia	Western virgins-bower	-	U	-	-	Buttercup
Collinsia parviflora	Blue lips	U	U	U	U	Figwort
Collomia linearis	Narrow-leaf collomia	U	U	-	U	Phlox
Commandra umbellata	Bastard toadflax	C	-	-	-	Sandalwood
*Convolulus arvensis**	Field bindweed	U	U	-	-	Morning glory
Corydalis aurea	Golden corydalis	-	-	-	U	Fumitory
Coryphantha missouriensis	Missouri ballcactus	U	-	-	-	Cactus
Crepis acuminata	Tapertip hawksbeard	U	-	-	U	Aster
Cryptantha celosioides	Northern cryptantha	U	-	-	-	Borage
Cymopterus bipinnatis	Hayden's cymopterus	U	-	-	U	Carrot
Cystopteris fragilis	Brittle bladderfern	-	-	-	U	Fern
Delphinium bicolor	Little larkspur	U	-	-	U	Buttercup
*Descurainia sophia**	Flixweed tansymustard	U	-	-	-	Mustard
Disporum trachycarpum	Wart-berry fairybell	-	-	U	U	Lily
Dodecathon conjugens	Slimpod shooting star	C	-	U	-	Primrose
Douglasia montana	Douglasia	C	C	-	-	Primrose
Epilobium angustifoliium	Fireweed	-	-	U	U	Evening primrose

* = non-native   **G** = grassland and shrubland   **T** = tall shrub draws
C = common   **R** = cliff and rock outcrops   **F** = forest and woodland
U = uncommon

Scientific Name	Common Name	G	R	T	F	Family
Erigeron cespitosum	Tufted fleabane	U	-	-	U	Aster
Erigeron compositus	Cut-leaved fleabane	U	-	-	U	Aster
Erigeron speciosus	Showy fleabane	-	-	-	U	
Eriogonum ovalifolium	Cushion buckwheat	-	-	-	U	Buckwheat
Eriogonum umbellatum	Sulfur buckwheat	U	-	-	U	Buckwheat
Eritrichium howardii	Howard's alpine forget-me-not	U	-	-	C	Borage
Erysimum asperum	Western wallflower	C	-	-	-	Mustard
Erysimum inconspicuum	Small wallflower	U	-	-	-	Mustard
Euphorbia esula*	Leafy spurge	U	-	U	-	Spurge
Filago arvensis	Fluffweed	-	-	U	-	Aster
Fragaria virginiana	Virginia strawberry	-	-	U	U	Rose
Frasera speciosa	Giant frasera	U	-	U	-	Gentian
Fritillaria atropurpurea	Checker lily/ Leopard lily	U	-	-	-	Lily
Fritillaria pudica	Yellow bell	C	-	U	U	Lily
Gaillardia aristata	Blanket flower	C	-	-	U	Aster
Galium boreale	Northern bedstraw	U	-	C	U	Madder
Gaura coccinea	Scarlet gaura	U	-	-	U	Mallow
Geranium viscosissimum	Sticky geranium	-	-	U	U	Geranium
Geum triflorum	Old man's whiskers/ prairie smoke	C	-	-	U	Rose
Gilia aggregata	Scarlet gilia	U	-	-	-	Phlox
Glycyrrhiza lepidota	Wild licorice	U	-	C	-	Wild licorice
Grindelia squarrosa	Gumweed	U	-	-	-	Aster
Gutierrezia sarothrae	Broom snakeweed	-	-	C	C	Aster
Habenaria unalascensis	Alaska rein-orchid	-	-	-	U	Orchid
Hackelia floribunda	Showy stickseed	-	-	U	-	Borage
Haplopappus acaulis	Cushion goldenweed	C	-	-	C	Aster
Hedeoma drummondii	Drummond's pennyroyal	-	U	-	-	Mint
Helianthus annus	Common sunflower	U	-	-	-	Aster
Hesperis matronalis*	Dame's rocket	-	-	U	-	Mustard
Heuchera parviflora	Small-leaved alumroot	-	-	U	U	Saxigrage
Hieracium albertinum	Western hawkweed	-	-	-	U	Aster
Hymenopappus filifolius	Columbia cut-leaf hymenopappus	U	-	-	-	Aster
Iris missouriensis	Blue flag	U	-	U	-	Iris
Kuhnia eupatorioides	False boneset	U	-	-	U	Aster
Lactuca pulchella	Blue lettuce	U	-	U	-	Aster
Lappula redowski	Western stickseed	U	-	U	-	Borage

* = non-native   **G** = grassland and shrubland   **T** = tall shrub draws
C = common   **R** = cliff and rock outcrops   **F** = forest and woodland
U = uncommon

Scientific Name	Common Name	G	R	T	F	Family
*Lepidium campestre**	Field pepperweed	-	-	U	-	Mustard
Lepidium densiflorum	Prairie pepperweed	U	-	-	-	Mustard
Lesquerella alpina	Alpine bladderpod	U	C	-	-	Mustard
Lewisia rediviva	Bitterroot	U	-	-	-	Purslane
Liatris punctata	Dotted blazing star	C	-	-	-	Aster
*Linaria dalmatica**	Dalmatian toadflax	C	C	C	U	Figwort
Linum lewisii	Blue flax	C	U	-	-	Flax
Linum rigidum	Yellow flax	U	-	-	U	Flax
Lithophragma parviflora	Smallflower woodlandstar	-	-	U	-	Saxifrage
Lithospermum arvense	Corn gromwell	C	-	-	-	Borage
Lithospermum incisum	Yellow gromwell	U	-	-	-	Borage
Lomatium triternatum	Nine-leaf lomatium	C	U	U	-	Carrot
Lupinus argenteus	Silvery lupine	U	-	-	-	Bean
*Medicago lupulina**	Black medic	U	-	-	-	Bean
*Medicago sativa**	Alfalfa	C	-	C	-	Bean
*Melilotus officinalis**	Yellow sweetclover	U	-	-	-	Bean
Mentzelia dispersa	Bushy mentzelia	-	-	-	U	Loasa
Mertensia oblongifolia	Oblongleaf bluebells	C	-	U	U	Borage
Musineon divaricatum	Leafy musineon	C	C	-	-	Carrot
Opuntia polyacantha	Prickly pear	U	-	-	-	Cactus
Orthocarpus tenuifolius	Owl clover	U	-	-	-	Figwort
Oxytropis lagopus	Rabbitfoot crazyweed	U	C	-	-	Bean
Oxytropis sericea	Silky crazyweed	C	-	-	-	Bean
Parietaria pensylvanica	Pellitory	-	-	U	U	Nettle
Paronychia sessilifolia	Stemless whitlowwort	C	-	-	-	Pink
Pedicularis contorta	Coiled-beak lousewort/ White coiled-beak	C	-	-	-	Figwort
Penstemon attenuatus	Sulphur penstemon	C	U	-	-	Figwort
Penstemon eriantherus	Fuzzytongue penstemon	U	U	-	-	Figwort
Penstemon procerus	Small-flowered penstemon	-	-	-	U	Figwort
Periderida gairdneri	Yampa	-	-	U	-	Carrot
Phacelia linearis	Threadleaf phacelia	U	-	-	-	Waterleaf
Phlox alyssifolia	Alyssum-leaved phlox	-	-	-	U	Phlox
Phlox bryoides	Moss phlox	-	-	-	U	Phlox
Phlox hoodii	Hood's phlox	C	-	-	U	Phlox
Plagiobothrys scouleri	Scouler's popcorn-flower	-	-	U	-	Borage
Polemonium pulcherrimum	Skunk-leaved polemonium/ Jacob's ladder	U	-	-	-	Phlox
Polygonum bistortoides	American bistort	U	-	-	-	Buckwheat

* = non-native   **G** = grassland and shrubland   **T** = tall shrub draws
C = common   **R** = cliff and rock outcrops   **F** = forest and woodland
U = uncommon

Scientific Name	Common Name	G	R	T	F	Family
Polygonum douglasii	Douglas' knotweed	U	-	-	U	Buckwheat
Potentilla concinna	Early cinquefoil	C	-	-	C	Rose
Potentilla gracilis	Slender cinquefoil	U	-	U	U	Rose
Ranunculus spp.	Buttercup	-	-	U	-	Buttercup
Ratibida columnifera	Prairie coneflower	U	-	-	U	Aster
*Salsola kali**	Russian thistle	U	-	U	-	Goosefoot
*Sanguisorba minor**	Burnet	U	-	-	-	Rose
Sedum lanceolatum	Lanceleaved stonecrop	U	U	-	U	Stonecrop
Selaginella densa	Compact selaginella	C	U	-	U	Spikemoss
Senecio canus	Woolly groundsel	C	-	-	U	Aster
*Sisymbrium altissimum**	Tumblemustard	-	-	U	-	Mustard
Sisyrinchium montanum	Blue-eyed grass	U	-	-	-	Iris
Smilacina racemosa	False spikenard/ Western Solomon-plume	-	-	-	U	Lily
Smilacina stellata	False starry Solomon's seal	-	-	U	U	Lily
Solidago missouriensis	Missouri goldenrod	C	-	C	-	Aster
Solidago multiradiata	Many-rayed goldenrod	U	U	-	-	Aster
Sonchus asper	Prickly sow thistle	U	-	-	-	Aster
Sonchus uliginosus	Marsh sow thistle	-	-	U	-	Aster
Sphaeralcea coccinea	Red globe mallow	U	-	-	-	Mallow
Stephanomeria runcinata	Runcinate-leaved skeletonweed	U	U	-	-	Aster
*Taraxacum officinale**	Dandelion	U	U	U	U	Aster
Thalictrum (occidentale)	Western meadowrue	-	-	U	U	Buttercup
Thermopsis rhombifolia	Round-leaved golden pea	U	-	-	-	Bean
Townsendia hookeri	Hooker's townsendia	U	U	-	-	Aster
Tragopogon dubius	Goat's beard/ salsify	C	-	U	U	Aster
Valeriana dioica	Northern valerian	-	-	U	U	Valerian
*Verbascum thapsus**	Mullein	U	U	U	-	Figwort
Vicia americana	American vetch	U	-	U	U	Bean
Viola nuttallii	Yellow prairie violet	C	-	U	U	Violet
Viola purpurea	Goosefoot violet	-	U	-	-	Violet
Woodsia oregana	Woodsia	-	U	-	-	Fern
Zigadenus venosus	Meadow death camas	U	-	-	-	Lily

GRASSES AND GRASS-LIKE PLANTS

Scientific Name	Common Name	G	R	T	F	Family
Agropyron caninum	Bearded wheatgrass	U	-	C	-	Grass
*Agropyron cristatum**	Crested wheatgrass	U	-	U	-	Grass
*Agropyron repens**		U	-	-	-	Grass

* = non-native G = grassland and shrubland T = tall shrub draws
C = common   R = cliff and rock outcrops F = forest and woodland
U = uncommon

Scientific Name	Common Name	G	R	T	F	Family
Agropyron spicatum	Bluebunch wheatgrass	C	C	U	C	Grass
Aristida longiseta	Purple threeawn	U	-	-	-	Grass
Bouteloua gracilis	Blue grama	C	U	-	-	Grass
*Bromus brizaeformis**	Rattlesnake brome	U	-	-	-	Grass
*Bromus inermis**	Smooth brome	U	-	C	U	Grass
*Bromus japonicus**	Japanese brome	C	-	U	-	Grass
Bromus pumpellianus	Pumpelly brome	U	-	-	-	Grass
*Bromus tectorum**	Cheatgrass	U	U	U	-	Grass
Calamagrostis	Pinegrass	U	-	-	-	Grass
Carex deweyana	Dewey's sedge	-	-	U	U	Sedge
Carex foena	Bronze sedge	U	-	-	-	Sedge
Carex geyeri	Elk sedge	-	-	-	C	Sedge
Carex petasata	Liddon's sedge	-	-	U	-	Sedge
Elymus cinereus	Great Basin wild rye	-	-	U	-	Grass
Elymus virginicus	Virginia wild rye	-	-	U	U	Grass
Festuca idahoensis	Idaho fescue	C	U	-	C	Grass
*Festuca ovina**	Sheep fescue (a cultivar)	C	-	-	U	Grass
Festuca scabrella	Rough fescue	C	U	-	U	Grass
Koeleria cristata	Prairie junegrass	C	U	-	-	Grass
Oryzopsis hymenoides	Indian ricegrass	U	C	-	-	Grass
Oryzopsis micrantha	Littleseed ricegrass	-	-	-	U	Grass
*Phleum pratense**	Timothy	U	-	U	-	Grass
Poa bulbosa	Bulbous bluegrass	U	-	-	-	Grass
*Poa compressa**	Canada bluegrass	-	-	C	U	Grass
Poa cusickii	Cusick's bluegrass	C	-	-	-	Grass
Poa interior	Inland bluegrass	-	-	-	U	Grass
*Poa pratensis**	Kentucky bluegrass	U	U	C	U	Grass
Poa secunda	Sandberg's bluegrass	C	U	U	U	Grass
Stipa comata	Needle-and-thread	C	-	-	-	Grass
Stipa occidentalis	Western needlegrass	C	-	U	U	Grass
Stipa viridula	Green needlegrass	C	-	U	U	Grass

* = non-native
C = common
U = uncommon

G = grassland and shrubland
R = cliff and rock outcrops

T = tall shrub draws
F = forest and woodland

MINERALS AND ROCKS FOUND ON MOUNT HELENA

MINERALS Augite
Calcite
Chalcedony (Agate, Jasper)
Dolomite
Chlorite
Glauconite
Galena
Goethite (limonite)
Hematite
Hemipnorphite
Hornblende
Illite
Malachite
Muscovite
Pyrite
Pyrolusite
Quartz
Talc

ROCKS Basalt
Breccia
Conglomerate
Dolostone
Hornfels
Limestone
Sandstone
Shale
Siltstone

FOSSILS Phosphatic brachiopods
Trilobites
Gastropods
Microorganisms
Trace fossils and pseudo-fossils (burrows,
    stromatolites, dendrites)
Mammals

MANMADE MATERIALS Brick
Glass
Lime
Potsherds
Quartz monzonite (building stone)
Rusted metal
Slag (melted and partially melted rock)

ABOUT THE AUTHORS

◆

Dan Sullivan is a Montana native who grew up along the Sun River near Great Falls. He received a Master of Arts in zoology and ornithology from the University of Montana. For more than thirty years, birds have found both a professional and avocational place in his activities. He serves as Montana's coordinator for the Breeding Bird Survey and is a member of the Montana Bird Distribution Committee which revised the fourth and fifth editions of P. D. Skaar's *Montana Bird Distribution*. He has been employed with the Montana Department of Agriculture for the past eighteen years.

Gayle Joslin is the Helena Resource Area wildlife biologist for Montana Fish, Wildlife & Parks. She received degrees in Wildlife Management and Zoology from Montana State University. A native of Helena, she has been exploring Mount Helena for forty years and now shares those experiences with her children. Interested in promoting the ethics of hunting, Gayle serves on the board of Orion—The Hunter's Institute.

Bea Vogel is a Montana native who has been collecting and studying spiders, butterflies, and other insects for over thirty-five years. She has a PhD from Yale University in arachnology.

Wayne Phillips, formerly a Forest Service ecologist, is now devoting his full time to teaching and writing about the flora of the Central and Northern Rockies. He has taught botany/wildflower classes at the Yellowstone Institute in Yellowstone National Park for fifteen years. His teaching experience includes botany classes as a faculty affiliate at The University of Montana, Montana State University-Northern, and the University of Great Falls. Wayne was a resident of Helena in the 1970s, and a charter member of both the Save Mount Helena Committee and the Mount Helena Run Committee. He now resides in Great Falls, but maintains an active interest in Mount Helena City Park.

Ray Breuninger is a geological consultant and a adjunct professor of geology and physics at Carroll College. In 1989 he and his family lived in Turkey, where Ray was a Fulbright Scholar. As an avid birder, natural historian, and longtime member of the Last Chance Audubon Society, Ray has led many geology field trips, and helped start Audubon's Natural History Lecture Series. He is currently laying out the trail system for Helena's Nature Park.

Erin Turner is a production editor at Falcon Publishing and has lived in Helena for two years. She has a degree in history from Grinnell College, Grinnell, Iowa, and has become an avid student of Montana's history.

Bonnie Heidel is botanist for the Montana Natural Heritage Program. An expert on the native plants of the state, she is responsible for overseeing information on rare species statewide. She is a Helena resident with a lasting regard for the neighboring wild residents.

In 1979 **Bill Schneider**, along with his partner, Mike Sample, created Falcon Publishing and released two guidebooks the first year. Bill wrote one of them, *Hiking Montana*, which is still a popular guidebook. Since then he has written eleven more books and many magazine articles on wildlife, outdoor recreation, and environmental issues. Along the way, on a part-time basis over a span of 12 years, Bill has taught classes on bicycling, backpacking, no-trace camping, and hiking in bear country for The Yellowstone Institute, a nonprofit educational organization in Yellowstone National Park. Since 1979, Bill has served as the publisher of Falcon, which is now established as a premier publisher of recreational guidebooks with more than 350 titles in print.

get
FALCON GUIDED

FALCON has **FALCON** GUIDES® to hiking, mountain biking, rock climbing, walking, scenic driving, fishing, rockhounding, paddling, birding, wildlife viewing, and camping. Here are a few titles currently available, but this list grows every year. If you would like a free catalog with an undated list of available titles, call FALCON at the toll-free number at the bottom of this page.

HIKING GUIDES

Hiking Alaska
Hiking Alberta
Hiking Arizona
Hiking Arizona's Cactus Country
Hiking Northern Arizona
Hiking the Beartooths
Hiking Big Bend National Park
Hiking California
Hiking California's Desert Parks
Hiking Carlsbad Caverns
  and Guadalupe National Parks
Hiking Colorado
Hiking the Columbia River Gorge
Hiking Florida
Hiking Georgia
Hiking Glacier & Waterton Lakes National Parks
Hiking Grand Canyon National Park
Hiking Hot Springs
  in the Pacific Northwest
Hiking Idaho
Hiking Maine
Hiking Michigan
Hiking Minnesota
Hiking Montana
Hiker's Guide to Nevada
Hiking New Hampshire
Hiking New Mexico
Hiking New York

Hiking North Carolina
Hiking Olympic National Park
Hiking Oregon
Hiking Oregon's Eagle Cap Wilderness
Hiking Oregon's Three Sisters Country
Hiking South Dakota's Black Hills Country
Hiking Southern New England
Hiking Tennessee
Hiking Texas
Hiking Utah
Hiking Utah's Summits
Hiking Vermont
Hiking Virginia
Hiking Washington
Hiking Wyoming
Hiking Wyoming's Wind River Range
Hiking Yellowstone National Park
Hiking Zion & Bryce Canyon National Parks
Exploring Canyonlands & Arches National Parks:
  A Hiking & Backcountry Driving Guide
Trail Guide to Bob Marshall Country
Wild Country Companion
Wild Montana

BEST EASY DAY HIKES

Yellowstone National Park
Canyonlands and Arches National Parks

■ *To order any of these books, check with your local bookseller or call FALCON® at* **1-800-582-2665**

FALCON®

BIRDING GUIDES
Birding Arizona
Birding Minnesota
Birder's Guide to Montana

FIELD GUIDES
Great Lakes Berry Book
New England Berry Book
Rocky Mountain Berry Book
Plants of Arizona
Rare Plants of Colorado
Willow Bark and Rose Hips
Tallgrass Prairie Wildflowers
Canyonlands Wildflowers

FISHING GUIDES
Fishing Alaska
Fishing Beartooths
Fishing Maine
Fishing Montana
Fishing Michigan

HOW TO GUIDES
Bear Aware
Leave No Trace
Wilderness First Aid
Mountain Lion Alert

PADDLING GUIDES
Floater's Guide to Colorado
Floater's Guide to Missouri
Floater's Guide to Montana
Paddling Oregon

ROCK CLIMBING GUIDES
Rock Climbing Colorado
Rock Climbing Montana
Rock Climbing New Mexico & Texas

ROCKHOUNDING GUIDES
Rockhounding Arizona
Rockhound's Guide to California
Rockhound's Guide to Colorado
Rockhounding Montana
Rockhound's Guide to New Mexico
Rockhounding Texas
Rockhounding Utah
Rockhounding Wyoming

MORE GUIDEBOOKS
Camping California's National Forests
Trail Riding Western Montana
Watching Wildlife
Wild Country Companion
Wild Montana

*To order any of these books, check with your local bookseller or call FALCON at **1-800-582-2665***

FALCON®

Scenic Driving Guides

Scenic Driving Alaska and the Yukon
Scenic Driving Arizona
Scenic Driving the Beartooth Highway
Scenic Driving California
Scenic Driving Colorado
Scenic Driving Georgia
Scenic Driving Hawaii
Scenic Driving Michigan
Scenic Driving Minnesota
Scenic Driving Montana
Scenic Driving New England
Scenic Driving New Mexico
Scenic Driving Oregon
Scenic Driving the Ozarks including the
   Ouchita Mountains
Scenic Driving Texas
Scenic Driving Utah
Scenic Driving Washington
Scenic Driving Wisconsin
Back Country Byways
National Forest Scenic Byways
National Forest Scenic Byways II
Traveler's Guide to the Lewis & Clark Trail
Traveling the Oregon Trail
Traveler's Guide to the Pony Express Trail

Wildlife Viewing Guides

Alaska Wildlife Viewing Guide
Arizona Wildlife Viewing Guide
California Wildlife Viewing Guide
Colorado Wildlife Viewing Guide
Florida Wildlife Viewing Guide
Idaho Wildlife Viewing Guide
Indiana Wildlife Vewing Guide
Iowa Wildlife Viewing Guide
Kentucky Wildlife Viewing Guide
Massachusetts Wildlife Viewing Guide
Montana Wildlife Viewing Guide
Nebraska Wildlife Viewing Guide
Nevada Wildlife Viewing Guide
New Hampshire Wildlife Viewing Guide
New Mexico Wildlife Viewing Guide
North Carolina Wildlife Viewing Guide
North Dakota Wildlife Viewing Guide
Ohio Wildlife Viewing Guide
Oregon Wildlife Viewing Guide
Tennessee Wildlife Viewing Guide
Texas Wildlife Viewing Guide
Utah Wildlife Viewing Guide
Vermont Wildlife Viewing Guide
Virginia Wildlife Viewing Guide
Washington Wildlife Viewing Guide
Wisconsin Wildlife Viewing Guide

■ *To order any of these books, check with your local bookseller*
*or call FALCON at **1-800-582-2665***

FALCON®

Mountain Biking Guides

Mountain Biking Arizona
Mountain Biking Colorado
Mountain Biking New Mexico
Mountain Biking New York
Mountain Biking Northern New England
Mountain Biking Southern New England
Mountain Biking Utah
Mountain Biking Denver/Boulder
Mountain Biking Moab

fat/trax Series
Bozeman
Colorado Springs